Local Small Business Marketing

by Alex Genadinik

ISBN:
ISBN-13: 978-1519556981

DEDICATION

Dedicated to my mother and grandmother who are the biggest entrepreneurs I know.

CONTENTS

FOREWORD

The advice in this book is based on my own experience and success promoting my business with the following local business marketing strategies and the success of many of my clients. In sharing these strategies, my hope is that you too will find success, and be able to grow your business using these techniques. I wish you the best of luck in your business and hope that the ideas in this book will hlp you. Enjoy the book.

Before we start

Hello, I am excited that you got this book, and I want to extend a very warm welcome to you. In writing this book I did my best to cover every element that I felt will help you get the most out of your local business marketing efforts.

GIFTS FOR YOU

In an effort to make sure that you get great value from this book, at the end of the book there are 3 additional resources that I made free for you. So check the back of the book for some extra freebies.

CHAPTER 1: INTRODUCTION

"Whether you think you can, or you think you can't, you are right."

- Henry Ford

1. What is a local business

A local business is any business that does business within some local radius or geographical limit that is typically no wider than the few nearest cities, with the limit often being narrower than that and as narrow as a few city blocks depending where most customers would realistically come from. For example, if you provide handyman services, even though traveling far isn't ideal, you might travel up to 60 miles to do a job, but if your business is a liquor store, most of your customers will come from no more than a few block radius surrounding your business.

Local services and local businesses can be anything from hair salons to construction and home repair, to restaurants to gyms to medical offices to laundromats to grocery stores, and *many* other similar businesses.

2. Why most local businesses are promoted similarly

Even though the businesses I just listed are all very different, surprisingly, about 80% (and sometimes much higher) of the marketing that you would do for those businesses is comprised of very similar techniques.

Let me explain this a little. These businesses all have websites, those websites all need to show up on Google search, all those businesses need to get professional and business referrals. They mostly need to get repeat customers, they have the same local media available to them to use for promotion and publicity, and they have many additional similar ways they can promote.

As you go through this book, if your business is a local business, you will see just how many of the strategies apply to your business without me ever knowing anything about your business other than that it is a local business or a local service.

3. Why offline marketing is still so effective

This book will cover both, online and offline strategies. I realize that most people these days are very focused on promoting their business on social media, SEO (search engine optimization), or through other online methods. These strategies do work fantastically, and I myself use them with tremendous success. But offline marketing can still get you very far, especially since most other people over-focus on online promotion of their businesses, it leaves the offline marketing techniques with less competition, which is great for you.

Offline marketing even has a number of strengths and advantages over online marketing. One of the main advantages that offline marketing has over online marketing is that in many of the offline marketing tactics, you get to meet people face to face, and forge a real human connection and a relationship. That is so much more powerful than having people find you online and click links, read text, see your little thumbnail photo, and at at best watch your video. So much of business is about relationships, and the offline strategies will help you develop your business relationships much more effectively.

In offline marketing, you can look people in the eyes, forge much stronger relationships, get people's trust, and have a chance to build a long-term business relationship with many people you meet. And not only will your sales conversion rate be higher after you get people's trust, but those new business relationships might give you value for years or even decades to come.

Some of the challenges that offline marketing has is that it doesn't scale like online marketing does. In online marketing, you can get hundreds, thousands, or even millions of people to come in contact with your work. But in offline marketing it takes a long time to talk to and convince many people to engage with your business.

Nevertheless, you can still accomplish quite a bit with offline marketing. It is still very effective, and in this book I will explain to you how you can get the most out of some of the most common offline marketing techniques.

4. Body language (nonverbal) sales communication

When you begin implementing many of the offline marketing and even some of the online marketing tactics in this book, you will immediately begin to meet many people in person, and talking to them. But did you know that up to 80% of all communication with your sales prospects can be nonverbal? In addition to communicating with the things you actually say, you also communicate with your body posture and positioning, your eyes, your hands, facial expressions, and the speed and tone of your voice, and even the way in which you are dressed?

Let's start with eye contact. Eye contact is something that subconsciously builds trust between people. Of course, don't be creepy with your eye contact and don't aggressively stare at people in the hope that you will build better eye contact.

Over-doing eye contact can make you seem strange, and can have a very negative effect on people, and put people off. Not having enough eye contact can make people feel like you are lying to them or that you are hiding something. But if you have just the right amount of positive eye contact, it can be very powerful during your conversations with people because it will subconsciously work to bring the two of you closer and establish more of a connection during your conversation with them.

Additionally, when you tell a story, and you get to some exciting or important part of that story, you can also emphasize the important parts of that story with the expressiveness of your eyes, which can often make your points and your storytelling much more effective. This is especially useful when you try to get people to imagine how much better your products or services can make their lives.

The next important aspect of your nonverbal communication is your body positioning and posture. Generally, you want to accomplish two things. You want to always appear open and comfortable. But you also want to mimic your sales prospect's body language. Salespeople often talk about mimicking voice, tone and body language of their sales prospects because it helps the sales prospects feel more comfortable and helps them get to like the salesperson since the salesperson is just like they are.

You should also be mindful of your overall energy level. If the person you are talking to is low-energy and maybe a little bit skeptical of doing business with you, you don't want to be too energetic. Instead, you want to come down to their energy level, and in a normal and calm conversation build trust and rapport. On the other hand, if the person you are talking to has a lot of energy and excitement, you have to match their energy and help them keep building up the excitement.

You should do the same mimicking and matching of your prospect's speed and tone of voice. People like other people who are just like them. They feel like those people are on their level, and subconsciously develop more trust towards them.

There are whole books devoted to nonverbal communication so there is a lot more to this. Nevertheless, these are your basic nonverbal body language tools to build immediate rapport with people you meet when you use many of the strategies that will be presented in this book.

5. Your business pitch

During your marketing and the day to day of simply doing business, you will be meeting many people and building rapport with them. The next thing to have in your marketing toolbox is a business pitch that clearly and effectively explains your business that you can use whenever someone asks you what you do, and what your business does (which will be very often).

When you talk about your company, you want to be brief and extremely clear. This helps people quickly understand your business and ask more questions if they are interested.

Here is a template for how you can explain your company very clearly at a high level in about 30 seconds or less. There are 3 to 5 main points you need to cover based on how much you want to divulge, and to whom you are talking.

1) I am (planning/started/growing) a company (fill in your company name)

2) Which is a (website? physical store? mobile app? restaurant?)

3) For (fill in your target audience here).

4) The company aims to (fill in what is the purpose of the company, or what does it do for the target audience)

5) By (explain what the company will do differently or uniquely)

Credit for template: This template comes from Adeo Ressi from the Founders Institute.

Here are a few examples of business pitches using this template.

Example for a restaurant: I am considering opening a high end Italian restaurant in downtown London because there are currently no such restaurants there, and mine will bring the unique and Italian flavor of Italy to the heart of England.

Example for a website: I recently launched a website for people who like to work on classic cars. The website has articles and videos with tutorials for how to work on cars.

Example for a gardening company: I am in the planning stages of opening a residential lawn care and gardening company in San Francisco which will focus on providing the best customer experience with the lowest prices.

Example for a technology business: I am in the planning stages of mobile apps company in New York. The company will create mobile apps that help people create business plans on their mobile devices.

See how simple and clear these pitches are? They aren't meant to get people excited about your company just yet. All they are meant to do is to clearly explain what you do so that the other person can understand what your business is, and perhaps ask follow up questions.

Also notice that some of the example pitches are just one or two sentences, and can be said in under 10 seconds so that the conversation keeps flowing. Now let me explain how to structure your sales pitch so that people get excited about doing business with your company, and actually buy from you.

6. Your sales pitch

If you want to get someone excited about doing business with you, and you want to aggressively (in a good way) pitch your business to them because they seem like a good candidate to become a potential customer, you must get them really excited from your very first sentence. Unlike your basic business pitch where you just have to make it clear what your business does, if you want to sell, you must also get someone excited about what they will be getting. When people buy, all they care about is what's in it for them.

Understanding this, the very first line of your sales pitch must be either some amazing promise (I will get to this in a second) or a qualifying question (I will get to this in a second also).

Let me explain what I mean by asking a qualifying question. This is a question meant to make whoever you are selling to feel like you understand what they need, and can provide the answer because you really understand the kind of a situation in which they find themselves in. Here are some examples:

If selling a weight loss product, the qualifying question would be: have you tried all the diets and exercise routines out there, but nothing has worked?

Most people would answer yes to that in their minds, and get more engaged with whatever you are about to tell them.

If selling a book about marketing to entrepreneurs, the qualifying question would go something like this: have you been trying to promote your business in different ways, but are just not seeing the results you had hoped for?

When making a sales pitch to people who have at least a tiny bit of patience, I like to start with a qualifying question. If I am making a sales pitch to people with absolutely no patience for any fluff, I immediately start with a big promise.

Now let me explain what I mean by making a big promise.

For example, if you are selling the same weight loss product, but want to come out with more of a bang with your pitch, and still be different enough from all the other products that didn't work, here is how your initial sentence might look like: lose 10 pounds in your first 30 days with our new research-based approach and the support of our trainers and dietitians who will create a unique program that fits your situation.

This may not be the best sales pitch opener in the world, but it accomplishes a few important things. It establishes credibility by noting research, and it expresses uniqueness in that the person will be helped with different kinds of professionals like trainers and dietitians.

If you are selling a marketing book, your initial opener can be something like this: this marketing book will give you time-tested and proven offline marketing strategies that will be effective in promoting your business and get clients.

Again, this isn't the greatest pitch in the world, but it does accomplish a few things. First, it offers a unique solution to a person's problem. Second, it establishes authority by offering proven and time-tested strategies.

By giving a big and unique promise as your very first sentence, your goal is to get the person interested enough to stick around to hear the rest of your sales pitch.

This is all a part of an age-old marketing tactic called AIDA which I will explain to you now. After learning about AIDA, you should use principles of AIDA with almost anything you try to sell in the future. It truly works, and you will get better and better results as you get better with AIDA after lots of practice.

AIDA stands for: Attention, Interest, Desire, Action.

In your sales pitch, you want to:

1) Grab a person's attention (A)
2) Then build and maintain their interest throughout your sales pitch (I)
3) As you keep their interest you should get them to desire whatever it is that you are selling (D)
4) The last part is for them to take action (A)

The first line of your pitch that I have been talking about so far is the "A" part of AIDA. This is where you must grab people's attention.

Now let's talk about keeping people's interests and inspiring their desires.

To keep people's attention and build their desire you must explain the BENEFITS and NOT FEATURES of the product or service that you are selling, and invoke their imagination and positive emotions.

Benefits (in the weight loss example) are things like losing weight, looking better, being sexier, and possibly even having more and better relationships after looking more attractive and being more healthy. These things are what people truly want. Features are things like diet plans, working with trainers and so on. No one dreams of having a diet plan. People dream of the benefit of their diet plan, which is to look better. And that is what you must focus on instead of the execution details.

The way you invoke people's positive emotions is by making them feel how challenging their current situation is, and helping them imagine how much better their lives would be after they got your product. Try to also use the word "you" as often as it can be used while still having your pitch sound well and make sense. The word "you" helps to get people to feel like your solution is truly for them, and begin imagining themselves getting the benefits of your product or service.

What we are talking about now is a field called Sales Copywriting. There are entire books on this subject. A well-written sales pitch can help you increase sales by hundreds of percent. Let me give you actual examples of videos where this kind of a script helped me raise sales by hundreds of percent.

Watch the sales video for my big online marketing course and see how I use the ideas I just explained in that video. This video helped me double the sales for this course overnight, and this course had already been selling well. The sales video should appear on top of the page here:

https://www.udemy.com/marketing-plan-strategy-become-a-great-marketer/

Here is another example of a video that helped me raise sales by hundreds of percent. The script for this video is exactly a model for the script of your own product or service. Use it as an example for how to craft your sales pitch:

https://www.udemy.com/how-to-create-grow-a-mobile-app-iphone-android-business/

If you need help crafting the pitch of your product or service, I can help you do that and increase your sales conversion. Just send me an email (listed at the end of the book) and I'll do my best to help.

Once you have gotten people's attention with your sales pitch, kept their interest and built up their desire, you must get them to take action. This action part is the last part of the AIDA process. It is the last A in the AIDA acronym. The action is often to buy something or to sign up for something. Instructing people to engage in the way you need them to engage is crucial. If you don't tell them what you need them to do, many of them won't do it. It is that simple.

If you take people through the AIDA path effectively, it will make your sales pitches work amazingly well for you. When I was first starting out with this, while it made sense in theory, it wasn't immediately clear how I can actually create such sales pitches on my own. But over time, I have become better and better with it, and so will you. Keep practicing it, and you will do great over time.

7. Key to your marketing success

I want to begin wrapping up this first chapter with just one quick note, mentioning that to succeed in almost any marketing strategy, you must have persistence and consistency. Whatever you try, if you are starting out, things might not always immediately begin working to bring you clients.

If at first things don't work, don't feel discouraged, and don't quit. Like all other entrepreneurs, you just have to persevere. Consistency and persistence will be the keys to your success. Keep trying to figure out what went wrong, and keep fixing it. Over time, you will find success with your marketing attempts.

8. Focus on retaining customers long-term

I realize that you may be very curious and excited about finding ways to get new customers. But did you ever hear a common business saying that it is easier to sell to an existing customer than it is to find a new customer?

Not only do repeat and long-term customers obviously spend more money with your business, but they help you in many additional indirect ways. Long-term customers are more likely to leave positive online reviews which will in turn help you draw more customers. Long-term customers are also much more likely to recommend your business to their friends, and many friends over time.

The common strategies to get people to become long-term customers are:

- Collect email addresses from your customers and write a regular newsletter with occasional announcements and discounts
- Have a multiple-product product line to let people buy additional products
- Have follow-on services for products people can buy like maintenance or part replacement
- Sell consumable products that are needed on a regular basis
- Sell subscription-based products or services
- Provide an amazing experience to your customers and delight them into coming back
- Provide great customer service that helps people build trust and positive emotions towards your business

9. Practical: how to get your business cards and flyers designed and printed

Later in this book I will cover how to promote your business with business cards, flyers and other print materials. You might wonder where to get these items actually designed and printed, so I'll cover a few options that you have.

If you want to do the design and printing online, I recommend a website called VistaPrint.com which is where I print my business cards and flyers. They have thousands of existing designs available that you can choose from. You can choose an existing design and get it printed for you right on that site.

If you want to have a custom design, you can do that on VistaPrint as well, although it will be a little bit expensive. To get a cheap custom design, take look at Fiverr.com where you can get business cards and flyers designed for you for as low as just $5.

Of course, as these strategies succeed for you and you will need to print more and more business cards, flyers and other printed marketing materials, you can approach local print shops to see whether they can work out a deal for a significant discount printing in bulk for you. The designs they can print can be the designs that you found on VistaPrint or got custom made on Fiverr.

Generally, the ultimate design is something that most people outsource because let's face it, most of us are not designers. It is easy to get the flyers designed for you and printed. The challenging part is to have what's printed on it resonate with people.

CHAPTER 2: ONLINE MARKETING STRATEGIES

"Social media is about sociology and psychology more than technology."

- Brian Solis

There are a few ways to get traffic online, and I will explain a number of those ways to you in this chapter. Some of the most common ways to promote your business are getting discovered when people search in Google, promoting on social media, and getting publicity if/when you do something noteworthy. That is the 10,000 foot view of online marketing. Now let's dive into more practical and specific advice for how you can leverage each of them in promoting your unique local business.

One thing that you should keep in mind is that online marketing is quite complex. Just think about everything you have to master or pay for if you want to do really well. You must find a great domain name, create a website, do SEO (Google search marketing) and social media marketing (Twitter, Facebook, Pinterest and others), generate publicity, do regular email marketing, master headline writing and sales copywriting, be able to choose the right strategies for growth, and much more.

All of this takes years to truly master, and outsourcing all of these things can get quite expensive. If you are a first-time entrepreneur, it can all be quite daunting. I'll do my best to help you understand what's necessary. Additionally, at the end of the book I offer a few free gifts to you, some of which are educational courses on how to do some of the above things. I truly want you to succeed, and this is why I am offering you additional educational resources. So please do take me up on my free gifts that I make available to all readers of this book.

Now let's start with our deeper look at online marketing strategies which you must get to work to promote your business.

1. Google SEO (search engine optimization) for your website

Getting your website to rank in Google search is very difficult these days because every business is trying to rank in Google, and that makes for a very competitive environment.

I recently had a client who started a moving company in San Francisco. The main search keyword that he needed to rank for in Google search was "moving company San Francisco" or "moving company in San Francisco."

As you can imagine, people who might be searching that phrase in Google are looking to hire movers and are pretty serious about it. No one searches that search just for entertainment value. Most people searching this phrase want to hire movers this month. Ranking for that term can bring many clients to a moving company so naturally some of the older and more established moving companies have paid tens of thousands of dollars to various SEO marketing agencies to get them to rank highly in Google search for precisely this term.

If you are a new moving company, it would be extremely difficult to rank in Google for such competitive searches in large cities with many potential clients and competitors.

I do offer free gifts at the end of this book, and one of those gifts is free access to my online SEO course that you can take for fee if you'd like. It will help you understand how to get your website to rank higher for Google searches that are relevant for your business.

While SEO is difficult, it is still possible to rank well in Google search. If your entire city is competitive as a whole, you can rank for searches in specific neighborhoods. That kind of a hyper-local strategy works for gyms, restaurants, medical offices and many other kinds of businesses which probably wouldn't even draw people from distant parts of their cities.

Here are the basics of SEO that you should be aware of. The most important thing is choosing the keywords that you need to rank for. The second part of SEO after you have identified the keywords is to create a website or pages on your website that would have a good chance to rank for those keywords. Lastly, after that website or web page is live, your job as the SEO marketer is to get it to rank in Google's top-10 search results and hopefully #1 in Google search results.

Mind you that there are entire books written on SEO, so it would be impossible to cover this broad topic in this small section and do it justice. This is why I am offering a free course on this. But let me try to unwrap the concepts that I just mentioned in a little bit more detail.

To choose the right keywords, you must think about what your ideal customers are searching. If you own a handyman business in Boston, very likely your potential customers are searching keywords like "handyman in Boston" or "fix broken door" or "fix whatever-it-is-that-you-fix in Boston" so if you can rank for those keywords, you would be very likely to get those searchers as clients because you can do exactly what they need done.

Once you identify the right keywords, you must use them throughout your website, and especially the title and description meta-tags of the pages which you need to rank in Google search.

To get these pages to rank higher in Google search, you must do two things. You can get other websites to link to your website (that helps your Google rankings) and you can constantly share your website and the pages you need to rank on social media.

You need to be doing all of this consistently over time. It usually takes months to rank a website in Google search so be patient, and keep learning and becoming better at Google SEO.

2. Yelp

Yelp.com is the world's largest local business listing site. It is free to add your company's listing there. Your listing on Yelp can also rank in Google search. The challenge you face with Yelp is that businesses which are your competitors are also on Yelp, and if you are just getting ready to post your business there, your competitors are probably already there ahead of you.

The main goal you should have for Yelp is to be the first or one of the first companies in your niche that comes up for relevant searches in order to get many customers from that site. If you are not one of the top businesses in your niche there, most people browsing the site will most likely just go to your competitors which are some of the top local businesses on Yelp in your industry.

To rank higher on Yelp, you have to do only two things. The first is to choose the right keywords for your listing title to go along with your name (do you begin to see a trend here? Keywords are a big part of much of online marketing) and get many 5-star reviews. With every 5-star review from your customers, you will get a chance to go up in Yelp rankings.

Since all businesses constantly work to get more reviews, some businesses bend the rules. As you can imagine, this is a big problem on Yelp, and they take many steps to curb such behavior. I would encourage that you familiarize yourself with Yelp's terms of service in order to maximize your reviews using strategies that are allowed under Yelp's ever-changing terms of service.

Overall, I would strongly encourage you to have a strong, long-term focus on Yelp because Yelp's listings often rank well in Google search, and millions of people search inside Yelp itself as well. It is a very trusted and authoritative site, so definitely allocate enough attention to it so that you can rank competitively in Yelp long-term.

3. Additional local business listing websites

Although Yelp.com is the biggest local business listing website overall, it isn't the most prominent such site everywhere in the world.

Many different cities, states and other countries have other local listing websites which are more prominent in those specific areas than Yelp.

Since I don't know where you are located, here is how I would recommend approaching this issue. Go to Google.com and search for your company's main search keywords in your city. Go through the first few pages of results and note all the local business listing websites to which you can add your own company's listing.

Long term, treat those websites just like you would Yelp. Keep getting good, 5-star reviews on them and make sure that your business is prominent there.

Some additional popular local business listing websites are AngiesList.com, thumbtack.com, yellowpages.com and a number of others. But again, see which are popular in your area, and focus on being prominent on those.

Additionally, whatever industry you may be in, there may be local business listing sites just for your industry. There is one for doctors, dentists, and many other kinds of local businesses. Make sure that your listing is very prominent there too.

Whatever local business listing website you decide to focus on, to be one of the top listings in your industry there you must get the keywords right, and long-term you must be able to get more legitimate 5-star reviews than your competitors and maintain a high overall rating.

4. Social media marketing for small business

Most first time business owners and first time marketers think that social media marketing amounts to posting promotional updates to Twitter, Facebook and a handful of other social media websites.

That kind of a basic approach typically does not amount to much success. Social media these days is much more about building, retaining, and re-engaging audiences. It is also about branding your business. For many companies these days, social media is also how they do much of their customer support.

You are probably most interested in how to get customers using social media so I'll start with that. As I mentioned, simply posting promotional links and messages typically falls flat on its face as a strategy. What works is building audiences. So how and where do you build an audience, and what does that really mean, anyway?

Today, building an audience can be done through your own blog, a YouTube show or a podcast that you create. You don't have to be a professional video or podcast creator when you start, but you should aim to become better and better at it as you move forward. Your blog, podcast or YouTube show concept can be on a topic that is close to your company's direction so that the people listening, watching and reading would be likely candidates to become paying customers of your business.

Of course, your aim with your blog and your show if you choose to create one is to get people engaging (reading, listening or watching) on a regular basis. Those would be called fans and because they obviously like what you are doing (why else would they be regularly watching?) you can sometimes invite them to subscribe to your email newsletter or check out your company's products.

As your presence on whatever large platforms that you chose to build an audience grows over time, you will also begin to stand out in your industry. This will work to make you seem more authoritative to potential clients and potential business relationships. It will help you increase sales because that extra authority will garner more trust which will translate into higher sales conversions.

So long term, you can make a significant amount of sales from social media directly by funneling your fans (people who are already familiar with your work, like it and trust you) to your products and indirectly by creating a stronger and more trusted brand, and generating more general recognition for your business. This isn't an overnight strategy, but this is a very sustainable and very strong long-term strategy that is head and shoulders stronger than trying to get some quick wins (and mostly not getting them) by randomly posting promotional messages on social media websites. In other words, this is a serious and professional strategy that will yield results.

To share my own experience with you, when I started on YouTube a few years ago, I had absolutely no clue about how to make videos. Even today I realize that I still have so much to learn. But over time I kept slowly (I wish it was faster in my case) improving. The more I improved, the more customers started coming to my business and to my product pages from YouTube, and the more recognition my overall work was starting to garner. It took a long time, but now I reach thousands of new people every day, and I wish/hope the same for you.

5. Google map listings for local searches

Let's focus on Google search a little more. Do you recall how every time you do a Google search for a local business like a restaurant or a store, or even the local Starbucks, Google always shows you a Google map in search results?

That Google map and the results on it typically show up at the very top of the first page of search results or close to the very top. Plus, the businesses that show up have their phone numbers listed there to make it easy for people to call, which makes it easier for those businesses to convert them into customers.

So, how about we get your business to rank in that Google map?!

It is actually relatively straight forward to do that in many cases. All you have to do is sign up for what Google calls "Google My Business" for free, by following this link:

https://www.google.com/business

After you go through the full sign-up process, Google will place your business listing in the Google map that shows up in search results when people search for relevant businesses. Keep in mind that it sometimes takes a week or two in order to fully complete the process because Google needs to verify your address.

If you are located in a busy area like a big city, there may be many businesses similar to yours which already show up in the map in search results. They might be difficult to displace at first. The way you displace and jump over those existing businesses is by, you guessed it, getting good reviews from your customers. Businesses that have more and better reviews typically rank higher than businesses that do not.

6. YouTube promotional videos & YouTube SEO

For my personal taste and experience with how effective this can be, this strategy is overall my favorite because you can make a relatively basic professional video on YouTube, do the SEO for it, and boost its views which will get that video to rank well in both YouTube AND Google search.

Let me explain how I do this and why it is so effective. This is quite an advanced technique to do correctly, but it doesn't have to be difficult.

Do you remember how we crafted your longer sales pitch in chapter one? That kind of a longer sales pitch is approximately what you should say in your YouTube sales video. And since this video is essentially you talking, you can produce it on your own from home in less than a day. I produce such videos in under 5 minutes because I already have a camera, a nice background, and a microphone. If you are budget sensitive, you can film such "talking head" videos with $99 software. I use software called ScreenFlow which cost me $99 and it works amazingly well. Once you get this software you don't need to buy a camcorder for producing basic talking-head videos. If you have a new computer and film in a quiet place, you can even get away without having a microphone. And a nice green screen for a professional background, and a stand for it should also cost under $100. You may also need to buy extra lights. In general, you can have an amazing home recording studio for under $200-300 that you can use to make money and promote your business with video for years to come.

You can use this exact setup for also producing your podcast or YouTube show in many cases.

In my case, this has paid back for itself tens of thousands of percent over, and even though I was price sensitive and skeptical of myself making videos at first, in hindsight I only wish now that I had made the right investments in equipment sooner.

Now that you understand how to make quality videos and what to say in them to generate sales, let me explain to you where the magic really happens.

The magic happens in a triple-play combination when you start promoting your video with my recipe to get views that I will now share with you.

Videos tend to rank higher on YouTube as they get more views. It is surprisingly cheap to get good views on YouTube by buying them from YouTube AdWords and since you know that the views are coming from YouTube AdWords, you are guaranteed that you won't be penalized (as you might if you buy views from other places where you have no idea where the views are coming from) and that the views are coming from real people. YouTube AdWords allows you to target who views your videos, and you can target people in your geographic area who might become your customers. As your video gets more and more views, it will start to rank well in YouTube for relevant searches, and over time possibly also in Google search for relevant searches.

This way you get the triple-play combination of views to your video from targeted views from YouTube AdWords, YouTube search and Google search. And all those views go to your highly converting video which is well-made and has a good script. This should lead to many clients over time!

I use this strategy and it is one of my favorite strategies because it is fast to implement, has proven to consistently get results when done right, and delivers those results quite fast when compared to other methods.

7. SEO Domination

You already understand that you can get your website to rank in the top-10 of Google search results. You also understand that you can get a YouTube video to rank in top-10 Google search results. You also understand that your Yelp or other local business website listing can rank in Google top-10 search results as well. And I hope you are already on your way to get your business listing to show up in the Google local business map results.

Do you see what is happening here? If you get all of this working for you, and continue on this path of using different websites with your content or listings on them, you can have almost all 10 out of 10 Google search results with your business on it.

This will crowd out your competitors and will surely make you one of the biggest (if not THE biggest) businesses of your type in your local area.

CHAPTER 3: BUSINESS CARD MARKETING & NETWORKING

Did you know what when first time entrepreneurs and marketers are asked about how they will promote their businesses, about 80% of them answer with something that is very close to this phrase:

"I will promote my business with business cards, flyers, Facebook and Twitter."

Be honest for a second, does this sound like your marketing strategy as well?

If it is, that is OK. Business card marketing is still a very powerful way to promote your business and begin many fruitful business relationships. It is also the one single marketing strategy you can continue to implement as you move through your daily life. Anywhere you are, there you can promote your business by striking up conversations with people and exchanging business cards with them.

Business card marketing and networking isn't just for networking events. If you are a business owner, it is a way of life.

In this chapter, I'll help you become as good as you possibly can with your business card marketing, and help you get as much out of it as you possibly can in the short term, and hopefully for the rest of your career.

WHAT YOUR BUSINESS CARDS SHOULD INCLUDE

1. What are you branding? Yourself? A business?

One of the very first things you should consider before even having your cards created is what you are ultimately trying to do with your business card marketing, and how it can best align with your overall business goals.

If your goal is to get clients, you must have your business cards and your pitch congruent with a similar message. Together they should work to lead people through the sales funnel that you choose. If you are not selling as aggressively, you might have more of a self-branded card with contact information.

But who are we kidding, if you are in business, you are always in sell mode!

This is why I recommend that you make two kinds of business cards, and carry a few of each type with you at all times. The first would be a sell-mode business card that you would give to people who you feel during your conversations with them, could become customers. The second type of business card you would create would be more of a generally branded business card which you can give to people if you don't think they would become a customer, but you would like to establish a general business relationship with them.

If having two kinds of business cards printed seems to you like overkill, just choose which kind of business card makes more sense for what you are trying to do. If you want to grow sales, I would recommend opting for the sell-mode type of business card. You will see how to make your business card more effective at sales as we walk through the other sections of this chapter.

2. Your name and catch phrase

The only things that you want to include on your business card with certainty at all times is you name and email address. All other information on your business card should be considered on a case by case basis depending on your business and what you hope to accomplish with that card. Let's go over what these other bits of information are, and which instances might be the right time to include them.

Right below your name, you might want to add your job title and/or catch phrase.

Your title might read like: "Founder and CEO" or "director" or any other plain job title. Many job titles tend to change over time so if you think yours might change in the next 6-12 months, you might want to keep the job title field relatively general so that any new job title you may have in the future doesn't make your cards obsolete in case you have hundreds of cards printed.

This is why you might want to include a catch phrase on your card. The purpose of a catch phrase is to make it very clear how you can help the people to whom you will be giving your card. In some cases it might be more effective to include a catchphrase than a job title, or at least incorporate your job title into your catchphrase.

For example, a catch phrase might read like "Top SEO marketer" if you want to get hired as an SEO (search engine optimization) marketer or consultant or "CEO of a mobile app development company X" if you want to get clients for your web development company.

For me, since I have written books, created my own mobile apps, coach entrepreneurs, and teach online courses, there can be multiple business cards, each with its own catchphrase.

For example, if I see someone over 45, knowing that older people tend to read more books and use less apps than younger people do, I might give them a business card that says "3-time Amazon best selling business author" and if I see someone under 25, knowing that younger people tend to get more excited about apps I might give them a business card with the catchphrase that reads like "creator of the Problemio.com mobile apps for entrepreneurs with over 1,000,000 downloads" although this catchphrase might be a bit too wordy. Plus, if the apps get to 10,000,000 downloads, it will obsolete my entire card.

Additionally, if during my conversation with people I learn that a person uses Udemy.com which is a website where people take online courses on just about any topic, I might give them a card with a catchphrase that reads like "Successful Udemy instructor with 50,000+ students and 60+ courses" although again, if I get to 100,000 students it might obsolete the card. Try to stay away from numbers like that on your cards unless those numbers are truly eye-catching and awe-inspiring. And if during our conversation I see that a person is looking for and appreciates business coaching, I might give them a card with a catchphrase that reads like "coached over 1,000 entrepreneurs."

Note about using numbers: as you can see, I have a tendency to use numbers in my catchphrases and headlines, and immediately second-guess myself. Let me explain why this happens and how you can remedy this. Headlines work better if you add numbers, percentages or statistics to them. That just helps them attract more attention. Over time I've trained myself to add numbers or statistics to make headlines more effective and impressive. Deciding on whether you will make use of this strategy is just the balancing act you have to play in weighing the pros and cons of what to include in your business card.

Not everyone should make so many different business cards, but keep in mind, **it is MUCH easier to sell someone something that they are already comfortable consuming**. My recommendation is to identify a few things you would like to sell, and make business cards that are most optimized to convert people who have a tendency to buy that exact thing.

For example, I wouldn't sell coaching or books to young people. And I wouldn't lead with my teaching on Udemy.com or the apps I made to older people, especially if they are not too familiar with the mobile world or Udemy. Instead, I would sell books to people who like to read, pitch my courses to people who already like taking video-based online courses, and try to sell my coaching to people who appreciate the value of it.

If you are brainstorming your catchphrase, feel welcome to email me and I can give you my feedback on it. It is one of the free gifts I offer readers of this book.

Even after you create a solid catchphrase, that catchphrase is just the beginning. You will see how the rest of the business card should develop in the next sections, depending on what you are trying to sell.

3. Your photo

When people talk to one another, they often incorrectly assume that they will remember all the details of that conversation an hour or a day after the conversation happens.

But the reality is that we forget most of what we discussed in a particular conversation. We even often forget what a person does and their face. This is especially true if we meet them at a networking event where we might talk to 10 or 20 people that evening.

Once a person can't remember what a business card they collected is all about, it will most likely end up in trash (hopefully recycling). One of the best ways to help people remember things about you is by adding your professional photo on the card. Your face will help them remember you, and that will increase the chance that they also recall more parts of the conversation you had with them, keep your card, and actually follow up by either emailing you, connecting on social media, or hopefully by entering the sales funnel which your card is designed to send them into.

4. Possible additional basic information to add

There are a few additional pieces of information that most business cards have that are almost a given.

Some years ago people would add their phone number almost automatically. But these days I would give that a second thought. Many people (specially younger people) no longer use the phone for talking. And when calls come in, they tend to be at random times, and interrupt whatever you are doing.

Depending on what you sell and the kind of a business you have, you might not want random people to call you. In my case, since I mostly prefer to funnel people to my digital products or connect on email or social media, I don't really want people to call me. Most of the time, that just interrupts whatever I am doing at the moment. I prefer that people either email me, connect on LinkedIn or other social media, or go directly to check out my products. Even though I offer coaching, it isn't my top sales priority so I stopped having my phone number printed on my cards.

Of course, for most businesses like local services, getting calls is a very important and welcome thing because it is the easiest way for those businesses to sell. If you want and need potential customers to call you, then by all means, go ahead and add your phone number.

Some people like to add their social media URLs to the card as well. The problem with that is that unless your business *is* social media in case that you might be a big YouTube star or a social media marketing consultant, it can be a weak way for people to connect, and it dis-focuses them from heading into your main sales funnel.

Unless you are a star on another social media platform, at most I'd suggest having your Twitter handle and possibly your LinkedIn URL.

One caveat is that if you have a very large presence on some social media website like maybe 100,000 Twitter followers or a Facebook page with 100,000 likes, or a YouTube channel with 10,000,000 views or something similar, it might be great to add a link to that because that is something that makes you truly stand out as the 99th percentile expert, and does wonders to give you a strong personal brand and make you appear authoritative, garner more trust, and have people be more likely to do business with you based on the increased trust and authority.

5. Link to your website or top of your sales funnel

A very important thing you want to add to your card is a URL of some sort. Most people just add their website URL and don't think twice about it, but there is a potentially better way to make use of the URL which you put on your card.

What I would recommend is that for every kind of card that you choose for your business and every kind of a product or service that you try to sell, try to send people to a unique URL that is optimized to sell that particular product or service. This also makes it easy to track the effectiveness of your business cards.

The same is true for the phone number which you list on your card. Some people buy unique phone numbers and print a different phone number on each type of card so that they can track which types of cards or other marketing techniques are generating most phone calls and eventual clients, and whether the overall business card marketing strategies are working for you.

Additionally, if you have a product on Amazon, Etsy, your own website, or anywhere else online that you want to send people to, you can post a URL-shortened link (after you put it through a URL shortener like Goo.gl or bit.ly) on your card so that people can go right to the product listing, and possibly buy that product.

You can add a call to action for the URL to your sales funnel like "Check out my most loved book" or "check out my best xyz" or "get immediate boost in xyz" to increase the conversion rate of people actually visiting that link. And after they visit it, it is up to your sales page and sales funnel to close that sale!

6. Make the card memorable by adding humor

Another way you can increase the follow-through of the people who collect your card is by adding humor. Most business cards are boring. So if your business card has a funny image (possibly on the back of it so as not to clutter the front of the card) that is on-brand and on-message with what you are doing, it can be a nice way to brighten that person's day, and make your card stand out to them at the same time.

They will certainly recall the nice feeling of laughter and associate that positive emotion with you and your business.

7. What not to add to your card

There are some things that you want to avoid while creating your card.

With all those great links to you product, social media, your name, catchphrase, and phone number, try to not clutter your card. I realize that you may be tempted to add as much information as possible. I am tempted by that as well so I fully understand you. But keep in mind that at some point there will be information overload, and the person to whom you are giving the card won't know how to best engage with you since they will be overwhelmed by the options.

Additionally, a cluttered business card is harder to read, which makes it less attractive to pick up and engage with. So having a cluttered design of your business card can greatly decrease the chances of having people follow up with you, and can cause you to lose potential leads.

8. Get professionally made cards

This should go without saying, but I'll mention it anyway since there will be some people who might make the mistake of trying to save some money by printing the business cards at home.

Do not print your business cards at home on regular paper. They will look very cheap, and if you go to a business networking event, it will literally be the worst card anyone collects that day because all the other cards they collect will be professionally made.

Professionally printing hundreds of cards is pretty cheap so make sure that yours are professionally made, and not home made.

9. Pros and cons of double sided business cards

There isn't a definitive answer for the best strategy for the back of the business card. So let me give you a few pros and cons for each argument so that you will be able to decide what's best for your unique situation.

If you leave the back of the business card blank, it can give space for whoever you give your card to, to write down some notes about your initial conversation. Granted, almost no one does this, but a few very diligent people do, and they will make good use of the business card.

Additionally, it is simply cheaper to leave the back of the business card blank. So if you don't have anything crucial to add to the back of the business card, perhaps just leave it blank.

But then again, since you are in business, how can you not have anything crucial to add? Of course you have at least something extra that you might want to add.

One example of a good use of the back of a business card is to add all of your social media URLs so that they don't clutter the front of the card. This can give people easy options to keep in touch with you, and also leave some room for notes on the back of the card if they want to make notes.

Another use of the back of the business card is to give people some sort of an offer. You might add a discount, or a few sentences about how some product or service of yours will greatly improve their lives, and then link to it. That is a pretty elaborate pitch for a business card, and while you would not have enough room for all of it on the front of the card, there is room for it on the back of the card.

The back of the business card might also be the place where you put more of your credentials, or something funny, or your photo if your photo didn't make it to the front of the card.

10. How to track your business card marketing results

After you give someone your business card, how do you know what they did with it? Most of the time you have no idea. You might assume they did something, but you have absolutely no proof of it unless you actually hear from those people. But most people don't follow up, so that still leaves you not knowing anything about what they did with your card.

There is one intelligent way to track how many people engage with your card, and even to what degree they engaged with it.

If on your card you either create a unique URL for people to visit, provide a unique phone number for people to call, or even better provide a unique product discount code or some free offer since people love free things and most people will engage with the free offer. Then whenever that URL, phone number or product discount code are used, you will be able to track that, and know that someone engaged with your business card.

This way, after months of business card marketing and networking, you will be able to know how much business this created for you. If you are happy with the results you've tracked, then just keep doing what you are doing. And if the results are not satisfactory, then you either have to do something about your pitch, your sales funnel, improve your in-person interactions and conversations, or perhaps choose other marketing tactics because this one might not be as effective for your unique business as you had hoped.

But at least by tracking, you will have a definitive answer.

11. How to make people keep your card longer

Discounts or x% OFF coupons on the card can make people feel like even though they don't need that product at the moment, they might want to come back to it at some point in the future. That will get people to put the card away instead of throwing it away (hopefully at least recycling) and hopefully coming back to the card at some future point.

12. Print your business cards for a discount at VistaPrint

VistaPrint.com offers your first batch of 200 business cards to be printed for a discount, and has a number of ongoing promotions almost at all times.

Full disclaimer: I am NOT affiliated with VistaPrint.

HOW TO ACTUALLY DO YOUR BUSINESS CARD MARKETING

13. How to do business card marketing

Now that you are equipped with a short business pitch, a long sales pitch, body language communication skills, and have the perfect business cards made for your business, you are ready to do some incredible business networking and business card marketing.

Networking is a lifestyle and a mindset. Wherever you are in any social situation, as long as you keep it socially appropriate, you are networking. Don't confine your networking to just networking events.

You should always have at least 3-5 business cards with you in your wallet. If you go to a networking event bring 30. If you present at a networking or business event, bring 50 business cards just in case.

Now let me explain how to make people want your business cards. Whenever you talk to people at networking events or any time in real life, don't just start going on and on about how great your business is, how much greater it will soon be, and what a great entrepreneur you are. And don't proceed to give people a business card right away.

Instead of being in an overly excited sell-mode (I understand how tempting it might be because I am constantly tempted to sell sell sell just as much as you are, but try to contain it just a little bit), what you must do is to first establish at least some sort of a relationship with whoever you are talking to.

One great way to begin establishing a relationship with someone you just met is to ask the person you are talking to about what they do for work. When they answer, listen actively, and follow up with insightful questions or suggestions for help or suggestions for people you can connect them with.

Let me give you a few guidelines on what to ask people to get them to open up to you, and build trust and rapport. Tap into people's emotions. We are all emotional beings (yes, even men are emotional). We all have hopes, aspirations, fears, anxieties, ambition, happiness, etc. What you must do is get out of the boring and bland fact-based conversations, and get into a conversation that leads people to happy emotions.

Here is an example of a question sequence that will have a very high chance to make you sound intelligent, get people to open up to you, associate their positive emotions to their interactions with you and your business, and build that immediate trust:

You: What do you do?
Other person: whatever job they do
You: what is your favorite part of your work? OR what inspired you to get into this?
(see how asking people what their favorite part of something is, and what inspired them will lead them towards something that they feel good about?)

Other person: some answer
You: what will it mean for you to truly succeed in what you do? Do you have a plan to get there?

(this kind of a question is meant to get them to daydream a little, and an answer would again tap into positive emotions)

Do you see how these questions you might ask are ones that tap into giving you more or less emotional answers which are positive? Also, almost no one asks those insightful questions. Most people just say something like "oh, you do xyz, that's awesome" which is followed by awkward silence.

Your conversation would be much more interesting and engaging. And after that exchange, the person you are talking to will want to know what such an interesting person as yourself does, and they will ask you what you do.

BOOM! Now is your time to shine. You already stand out above the crowd to the person with whom you are talking. Now, just give a brilliant pitch of your business to make you and the business look like a million bucks (remember making your basic business pitch in chapter one?). Give them a way to engage with your business if there is any synergy between the two of you (if not, then what are you still doing there at that point?), and suggest exchanging business cards if the other person hasn't already suggested exchanging business cards.

Let me give you a few tips for what to do with business cards that you collect. Carry a pen with you so that as soon as you step away, you can write down some of the key points of your exchange with the person with whom you just talked to, and what you must follow up about. Within the next 30 minutes, you will forget half of the conversation you just had, and by the next day you will forget even more. Taking a few quick notes will go a long way in helping you retain the important points about which to follow up.

Ideally, the next day after meeting, you should email them to build on your conversation, and suggest next steps for the two of you if there are any that make sense.

As a rule of thumb, always follow up in the next day or two on every business card that you collect. Also, try to follow your new contacts on Twitter or connect with them on LinkedIn. Those are the minimal things you can do to keep in touch, and create positive long-term business contacts.

14. PRO tip: outdoor/vehicle business card holder and dispenser

One very nifty thing you can do is buy a business card holder for your car and/or storefront. These are little and very inexpensive low-tech tools that stick (or somehow get attached to) to glass. They are meant to be outside your store or your car so you don't have to be present to have someone take your card.

They only stick out about an inch or so, so it wouldn't interfere with anything, but it would enable you to let people take your business cards if they walk by your storefront and don't necessarily walk in, or if they see your logo on your car and become interested. This way you can be giving out business cards at any time, even if you are sleeping.

If your business is closed, people can still take your card from your storefront, and if you are away from your car, people can still take a card from your car.

15. Collect business cards, follow up AND put into new contacts email database

You already know that you should follow up on the business cards that you collect. But there is another thing you can do with those cards.

Independent of actually following up on the business cards that you collect, you should also put people's names and emails into your own mailing list that is made up just of people whose business cards you've collected.

Don't abuse that mailing list by sending sales emails to it all the time. But do make a separate email list for those contacts to keep in touch with them. They've met you in person, and might be OK with getting occasional updates from you, and even occasional announcements for sales or product launches.

16. Business card mobile apps (save trees)

There are many mobile apps for Android and iPhone that you can use to scan business card information, and store that information. This way you don't have to collect the actual business card from people you meet, save them the few pennies of having it printed, and save the paper (and trees) that were used to make that business card.

Additionally, these kinds of business card apps also help you organize contacts so if you have a tendency to mismanage or lose the business cards you collect, these kinds of apps can help you stay on track.

17. Follow up in unique and creative ways to be memorable and stand out

Remember, the goal isn't to give out your business cards and to collect the cards of other people. That is all just a step in the right direction.

The real goal is to establish business relationships and hopefully get clients through your business card marketing efforts. And how do you get clients and make people want to have business relationships with you? By following up in the best and most professional way that you can, and to stand out as a quality professional.

If you have a big sales prospect, maybe send them something by snail mail. I don't personally do this, but many people report feeling appreciation when they receive something like this. If you want to follow up by email, make it a pleasant one, and add something of yours that they might appreciate for free or at least with a very big discount. Try to do something nice and unusual to stand out of the crowd.

CHAPTER 4: FLIER MARKETING

1. Why marketing with flyers is still so effective

There are so many cool ways to promote your business like social media marketing, YouTube, SEO (search engine optimization) and many other online and offline techniques. So, why is flier marketing still so effective?

The answer lies in two general truths. The first is that people still often prefer to have something in their hands that they can touch, feel, save on their desks or shelves, and come back to when they are ready. They can save the flier in case they don't necessarily need it right there and then, but think that they might make use of it later. The second reason flier marketing is still so important is a little bit more practical. It is that YOU decide who gets the flier, and there are various levels of complexity for how you can decide on, and hone in on the most ideal people to whom to give your flyers. Precisely this hyper-targeting of your potentially ideal clients is what often makes marketing with flyers so effective.

2. Demographics, psycho-graphics and geo-targeting

What are these fancy terms? Let me define them for you.

Demographics: measurable attributes of your target customers like age, sex (not "yes please" but male/female), education level, income level, where they live and the affluence of that neighborhood, their political affiliation, and many additional concrete and measurable attributes.

Psycho-graphics: these are not measurable but still important attributes about your target customers. These are things like interests, hobbies, needs, fears, desires, hopes, insecurities, things they feel that they are lacking and need in their lives.

Geo-graphics: this is basically where these people live. For many local businesses, you must find customers who are local and live within a certain radius.

Now let's explore how you can identify the demographics, psycho-graphics and geo-targeting of your most ideal potential customers to whom you will give your flyers.

3. Understanding your customers

How well do you understand your customers? Do you know them better than they know themselves? Ultimately, you should work to be able to say yes to that. After all, once you know what they need, want and like better than they themselves know what they need, you will be able to make a product that amazes and delights them, and you will be able to package and promote it in a way that makes them desire and salivate over it.

But I may be getting a little bit ahead of myself here. Let me start with the basics. When most first-time business owners are asked who their ideal customer is, the most common answer they give is "everyone."

Now let me ask you, who is your ideal customer? Is your answer something like "everyone" or "all women" or "all men?"

If so, it is OK, but we have a little bit of work to do to refine it. I know that you would take anyone as your client. I would too. But there are some people who are most ideal candidates to become clients. I don't know what your business is, so let me give you a few examples so that you can try to apply it to your unique situation.

If you sell a high-end product which is expensive, most likely your ideal customers will be more educated, have extra discretionary income to spend, and have more refined tastes. They could also be older since older (over 35 or 45) people typically have more money to spend. They might also want to uphold to a certain social status and chase what their friends are buying.

If you own a fast food restaurant, your customers might be younger people and people who have less money to spend.

They could also be students at a nearby school or college. Discounts and promotions may appeal to them more.

If you own a high-end restaurant, your target audience might be people over 30 years old with refined tastes who may want to impress the people with whom they are dining.

If you have a fashion boutique, you most likely attract women who like certain types of fashion. That fashion is typically worn by certain age groups with specific lifestyle traits that you can deduce from that specific fashion.

Let me give you an example of the ideal customers for a part of my business. That part of my business is an Android app that helps entrepreneurs plan their businesses, and generally learn how to get started with their business. Here is the app. It is free if you'd like to check it out:

https://play.google.com/store/apps/details?id=com.problemio

I'll tell you exactly who downloads this app. The download rate is approximately 60% male and 40% female. The audience is 40% in US, 5% in Canada, 5% in UK, 4% in Australia, 5% in South Africa, 10% in India, and the remaining users are all over the world. They are usually under 30 years old, and a significant percentage of them are under 25 and 20 years old. Most of the users have never started a business. The kinds of businesses they most often want to start are local service businesses, meaning they often need to raise money which they have a hard time with. Very few of them ever get actually started with their businesses, but the reason they mostly get the app is to write a business plan for their business, presumably because since they can't actually start the business, planning it is the biggest thing they can do.

Do you see how well I know my users? I know much more about them than I wrote. I just had to limit what I share about them so that you don't get bored reading about it since you probably don't care and get the point I was trying to make. Try to think about what your ideal customers are like. This way you can craft the best offer and product for them.

You might wonder how you can get to know your ideal customers, and the answer is actually very simple. Just talk to people who you think are your potential customers. Ask them about their wants, needs, and what they would most like to see from your product or business. Talk to them every chance you get and truly listen.

4. How to begin understanding your customers

When first starting out, entrepreneurs tend to make many assumptions about their future customers. But assumptions usually lead people astray. That's why the absolute best way to get to know your potential customers and their wants and desires is simply to talk to them.

How do you think I know so much about my app users? I have talked to over 1,000 of them over time. Various analytics software only told me where they come from, but as for all the other information, that I got from talking to many of them.

You must constantly talk to your current and potential customers about what their needs are, their experience with your business, and how your product can help them more and better. Over time you will get to understand them on a much deeper level, and you will be able to create offers that truly resonate with them and get them excited.

5. Types of businesses that get best results with flyers

While if you are creative and resourceful enough in how you do your promotion, you can probably successfully promote any business with flyers, some of the best types of businesses to promote with flyers are local businesses and events because you can geographically target people when you hand out the flyers.

Businesses that tend to be difficult to promote with flyers are ones which don't make a significant amount of money per customer and rely on reaching a large scale of low-spending customers to reach high revenue numbers. Since flyers have a cost to printing and handing them out, unless you can make a significant amount of money per each signed-up customer, it will lose you money because typically you have to hand out many flyers to generate a single sign-up.

6. What does your customer really think?

When you create your business, logo, website, and everything else, a large part of your motivation is to grow your own personal success, brand, and improve how you are seen by others. 99.9% of all people are generally most motivated by improving their own situations.

Understanding this, what do you think your customers care and think about when they come in contact with your flier or your business?

All your customers want to know is "what's in it for me?" so when you create your flyers, create the flyers out of understanding that this is how people will approach your flyers. I'll explain how to create your flyers shortly, but for now just think about this.

HOW TO DESIGN YOUR FLIER

7. 4 elements of an great flier

There are 4 things that should be present in every effective flier. In coming sections of this chapter I will explain how exactly to create each of these sections for maximum effect and conversion. For now, let me just explain what each of those four elements is.

The most important element is your offer. It must excite people by being so compelling, and grab people's attention and gets them to stop in their tracks and take a look.

The second element of a well crafted flier is the photo. You should have one large and clear photo. The photo should communicate what the benefit of your business is, and inspire people to imagine how great it would be for them to get the benefits of your business.

The third element that every well crafted flier should have is the call to action. You must tell people to call or visit or engage with your business in whatever other way that makes sense.

The fourth element of a well crafted flier is the extra details section that expands on, supports and explains your main offer. Those details should drive the point home about how great it would be to get the benefits of your business.

8. AIDA for your flier

The first element is AIDA is the A which stands for attention. In the real world, what grabs people's attention is the headline of whatever ad you are creating. In the case of flyers, the A or the headline is the offer on your flier. The offer must be so good that it stops people in their tracks. If the offer is mediocre most people won't take too much of an interest.

The next part of AIDA is the I which stands for interest. Once you have people's attention with your headline, that attention will only last a few seconds unless you build on it. The way you build people's interest in your flier is with your photo and the extra offer details that you add below the offer.

The next part of AIDA is D which stands for desire. This is crucial. People's interest must turn from theoretical and vague interest to true emotional desire for whatever it is that you are offering. After grabbing people's attention, building an emotional desire in them is probably the second most crucial element in your sales. In fact, after you master headline writing, the element of AIDA with the most depth which truly takes a lifetime to master is the process of turning people's interest into a true emotional desire.

After people's emotions are involved and they truly desire your product, they will do the rest of the work for you by convincing themselves just how much they need whatever it is that you are selling.

Once you really get people to desire your product, the last part of AIDA is the last A which stands for action. You must get them to take action, which is to buy something or call your business or sign up for something in some way, whatever that may be for your particular business.

Now we are ready to walk through the elements of a successful flier in more detail, with AIDA in mind.

9. How to create an amazing offer (the A in AIDA)

Your offer is the A of AIDA, and it must grab attention. Creating a great offer is easy in theory. If you offer something for free or at an incredible discount, people will flock to your unbelievable offer in droves.

The problem with doing such an offer is that it will lose you a significant amount of money.

The key to being able to realistically give such a great offer is to be able to make a significant amount of money on average per each person that takes you up on that offer by converting enough people to becoming lucrative long-term customers.

For example, if you are promoting a gym, you can give away a pretty significant free membership trial just to get people to take you up on that offer. Most gyms give one free class to try for free, but what if you gave away 10 classes or 10 free days? That would certainly get people's attention much more. Using the same gym example, if you significantly reduced initiation fees much more than people typically expect, that would also get people's attention.

The trick is that if a person signs up, some people might remain members for many years, which would get you thousands upon thousands of dollars from them. And if they love your gym they might also get personal training, buy some of your gear and workout clothes, and even make you more than $10,000 over the lifetime of their membership.

By getting their attention, you increase the chance of that $10,000 client happening vs. not happening at all.

So whatever business you have, you must refine and improve your long-term customer strategy and make sure that you can make a significant amount of money per customer. Once you have a large LTV (lifetime customer value) you can make your attention grabbing headlines more and more attractive, while still being profitable and sustainable long-term.

So if you are own a gym, you must get people to remain members for a long time. If you own a restaurant, you must get people to order or visit from you many times. If you own a cleaning or a gardening business, you must get people to use your business on a regular basis. For almost all kinds of businesses, what this really boils down to is simply making sure that you provide a consistently great service at a fair price. That will get many people to become long-term customers, which will enable you to give more attractive offers to get people's attention.

Additional tips to write more attention-grabbing headlines involve using words like FREE or giving a x% OFF (some percent off) discount or $x OFF (some amount of dollars off) discount. Try to also use numbers in your headlines. That gets more attention too.

10. What kind of a photo to choose

The photo you choose for your flier should help people build their interest in your business, and the image in the photo should get people to begin imagining themselves getting the benefits of whatever it is that your business offers, and how much better their life will be after getting what your business offers. This will help to transition them to true emotional desire for your product after they truly imagine themselves getting all those amazing benefits, and how much better their lives would be after getting the benefits of your business vs. not getting those benefits.

The photo must inspire their imagination.

11. Extra information and details (I and D of AIDA together with the photo)

Under your headline offer, you should also have a few (maybe three) bullet points that further expand on your big headline offer. Use those extra details to list *benefits and not features* of your product or service. This will work together with the image that you choose to get people to imagine having those benefits in their lives, and begin to desire those benefits.

Together, these extra product benefit details and the photo are your I and D (building of interest and desire) of AIDA.

For example, if you are promoting a gym, some of those benefits might be things like quickly losing weight, looking better, wearing an attractive bathing suit on the beach, or many other common benefits that a gym ultimately offers. Those benefits have been promised to us by people for decades because they work to get people imagining and desiring to be like the people in the pictures.

12. Call to action (the last A of AIDA)

After people desire your product or service, you must make sure to close the deal and get those people into the doors of your business. You do that with an effective call to action which is the last A of AIDA, and the fourth element of a successful flier.

To make your call to action more effective you can add urgency to it by either limiting the total number of products available in that offer or the time during which the offer on the flier is valid.

For example, you can urge people to call this weekend (or week or month) because the offer expires after that. Or you can say that only x number of people get the offer, and they get it on a first-come-first-serve basis. These kinds of things are designed to get people to act on the offer instead of filing it away and forgetting about it.

13. How to get flyers made (cheapest to expensive)

Now that you know how to design all the necessary elements of your flier, it is time to get them printed.

It might seem that the cheapest way to print the flyers is on your home printer. Doing this will give you low quality flyers which will be on basic flimsy paper. It isn't great, but at least it is a start.

Of course, cheap looking flyers will have a far lower conversion rate. So you would be well advised to get the flyers printed at a local print shop or on vistaprint.com as I mentioned earlier. If you are resourceful you can negotiate a discount with a local print shop or find discount deals on vistaprint.com, and it might end up being even cheaper to print flyers that way instead of printing them from home.

There are a few types of flyers that you can print. They can be business card size, postcard size, fold-out brochure type of flyers, or hang-on-door types of flyers which you can hang on people's doors instead of having to slide them on the floor under their doors if that is one of the ways in which you distribute the flyers.

14. Mistakes NOT to make with your flyers

Do you remember the section of the book that talked about what your customers are thinking? Remember how all your customers care about is what's in it for them?

Whatever isn't for them, don't add that to your flier. For example, do you think they care about your logo? They don't really care. Do you think they care a whole lot about you? I am sorry to say that they don't. You are a feature of the product or service but you are certainly not a benefit. They will care about you a little bit later in the sales process, but they don't care about you when looking at the flier.

So don't add your logo or too many details about you or your credentials just yet. Instead, add what you can do for them, and the benefits you will give them. Try to take out all the unnecessary information from the flier because it will just create clutter and confusion. And every little bit of increase of clutter and confusion in the flier will decrease its effectiveness.

Your customers will never tell you why they didn't call you and why they didn't engage with your business. They will ignore you in silence. So you must be proactive in understanding the reasons why they might not engage, and not make those mistakes.

HOW TO DO YOUR FLIER MARKETING

15. Who should hand out the flyers?

Long-term you will, of course, hire someone to hand out your flyers because you have a million other things you need to do for your business, and don't have time to stand there and hand out your flyers.

But when you first start out, it is very important that you hand out your flyers, and if you really want to hustle (which I know you do) it might be a good idea to spend an hour or two every few weeks handing out your own flyers even as your business matures.

Handing our your own flyers will help you see how people react to your product offer, and you will even be able to chat and interact with some of the people to whom you hand the flyers. Those conversations are invaluable because those people will explain to you exactly why they do or do not take an interest in your flier, and that will give you further ideas for how you can improve your flier design and overall flier marketing.

Those insights and ultimate improvement in your flier design will boost your flier marketing results and give you more customers long-term. Doing this will make your overall flier marketing more effective and profitable.

16. Where you can hand it out or post flyers

You may already have some ways in mind for handing out your flyers, but let me quickly list a number of ways in which you can distribute them. Hopefully it will give you some additional ideas to the distribution strategies you already have in mind.

While you can obviously hand flyers out on the street, you can also put them under people's doors in their homes and apartment buildings. You can also get the hang-on-door flyers made and hang them on people's door knobs to get more attention than just sliding them on the floor. You can also buy outdoor flier dispenser trays that can stick to glass so that people can take them when your business is closed or if they are just passing by on the street and don't necessarily walk in. You can also approach other nearby businesses and ask them if you can leave your flyers on display in their store. This usually works if you offer to display their flyers somewhere in your business. You can also give flyers to people at the point of purchase. Those flyers can have additional discounts for next purchases. This would incentivize people to come back to your business to redeem the discounts on those flyers. You can also go to neighborhood and community events and try to distribute the flyers there. You can also put flyers on the windshields and side windows of cars. You can also post your flyers on community billboards and bulletin boards, and on neighborhood street posts where people post announcements. Lastly, you can mail the flyers by snail mail to people who live in the neighborhoods which you target with your geo-targeting.

17. How to track effectiveness

I already alluded to tracking the effectiveness of your flyers earlier in this book, but since this is an important topic, it is worth covering it again with more focus.

If you don't have a way to track effectiveness of your flier marketing campaigns, you have no idea whether it is profitable or whether it is worth doing in the future. It is like shooting blind or in the dark. That is a very bad strategy because for all you know, you can be wasting your time and money.

The professional approach would be to enable yourself to track the results of your flier marketing. The way you would do that is to give a unique email, phone number, discount code, or website URL (some page on your website with a discount offer) that only people who take the flier would know about. This way you can tell whether the flyers are generating leads, and then track which of those leads become paying customers. Over time you would be able to track how much revenue and profit those customers brought your business over the long-term, and be able to calculate whether the total profit from those people covered the cost of your flier marketing campaign.

That is the only way you can determine whether the flier marketing campaign is actually financially viable long-term or whether you are losing money on it.

But once you find a flier design that converts well and generates many leads to your business that then convert into paying long-term clients, you will have an absolutely winning long-term formula for the lifetime of your business that you can use to grow and expand as much as your heart desires!

CHAPTER 5: EVENT & WORKSHOP MARKETING FOR YOUR LOCAL BUSINESS

Events or workshops can be an amazing way to promote a local business. Events give you extra ways to get exposure and publicity for your business. They also give you a way to funnel leads to become clients of your main business. And the best part about having your own event series is that it can also be an extra revenue source for your business.

In this chapter I'll explain to you how you can create a successful event series of your own, and use it to promote your business and generate extra revenue.

1. My story and case study of how I created a successful event series

How do I know about starting a successful event series? Well, years ago I naively started a business which was essentially a group hiking website. Every hike is essentially an event that required its own organizing, planning, marketing and a way to generate sufficient revenue. We'll touch on all of this as we go through the book.

My hiking business turned out to be my first reasonably successful business, but how I got it to be a success was very far from a straight line. It was an incredible struggle before I saw any sign of success.

If you are curious to take a look at what the business once was, even though I don't currently run this business, the website is still up at:
http://www.comehike.com so that you can get a sense for what the business was.

As you can see from the website, it was quite an amateur effort. But despite that (and in a sense despite myself and my beginner mistakes), later in this book I'll explain how the business became a success.

But first, let me explain to you the mistaken initial business strategy I had for this business, and what I later identified as my biggest errors. I thought that people hate event websites like meetup.com because the organizers have to pay a monthly fee. So I thought I would make money by keeping my site free, and by publishing ads on my website. In my mind this would give event organizers a free option to manage their hikes, and for that reason they would flock to my website and leave meetup.

My main mistakes (there were many smaller ones not worth mentioning yet):

1) The ad revenue model only works for websites with a LOT of traffic because on average my Google ads (AdSense ads) made $6 per every 1,000 page views. This means that even if I got 100,000 monthly page views I would only be making $600 which isn't even enough to pay half of my rent. And to make a decent American middle class salary of $6,000/month I would need 1,000,000 page views each month which is very difficult to do for such a small niche website. So the monetization strategy was too weak for the kind of business that this is.

2) My second mistake was competing with a thriving, loved and growing established website like meetup.com because it proved very difficult to get hike organizers to switch to my website from Meetup because Meetup had so much more quality and tens of thousands of hikers, which my website obviously did not.

3) Poor website design and branding which you can immediately see by visiting comehike.com - this also hurt the growth of my business.

Since I made so many obvious mistakes, the one thought that haunted me for years after having started this business was that if I had a mentor or a good advisor, in literally 5 minutes of conversation they could have steered me away from those mistakes, and that would have saved me money and many months of struggle.

But that struggle that I had to go through to "wiggle out" of my mistakes was what allowed me to create a great outdoor event series that went from a total disaster to being talked about on NPR (National Public Radio), generating a significant amount of money, getting me a lot of publicity, and ultimately making this business as successful as it could have been.

As this chapter moves forward, especially later when I discuss event marketing, I will also share what happened in my own event series at different times, so that you will see the case study of my own experience and hopefully will be able to apply it to your events to avoid big mistakes on your path to success.

2. The basics of creating a successful event series and what you need to keep in mind

The biggest thing that will help you is consistency over the long term. People almost never get it right from their very first event (or first bunch of events if you are like me). There are many things that have to fall into place like marketing, event quality, and many other factors. It simply takes time to get all the details right.

My own event series, when it first started, would get zero or just a handful of attendees. If I had used that as a sign to stop, I would have never found the success much later.

So even before you start your first event, try to focus on the long-term, and position the event series as a long-term project for you. That way you will refine the problems over time, and after lots of trial and error you will get it right, and find success. But it will only come from *consistency*.

So if you don't get great results at first, don't be discouraged. That is a common phenomenon. Just keep hacking away at it to correct what went wrong.

Another common thing you must figure out for your event series is the balance of price vs. growth. Obviously if you make events free, you will draw maximum attendance, but even if you start charging even as low as $1 you will immediately and significantly decrease attendance. So you always have a balance between growing attendance as aggressively as possible vs. making money from the events. I will cover how to manage this later in this chapter so that you can have the most growth while making the most amount of money.

Here is my **3-part formula for having a successful event series**, and almost any other business. It is like a 3-legged stool where all 3 legs have to work. If one leg of a stool doesn't work, the stool falls, and in case of the event series, it doesn't succeed. So the three "legs" are:

1) marketing and growth
2) event quality
3) it has to make sense financially, and generate you enough revenue to meet your financial goals for the events

Always have these most important aspects in mind when thinking about your event series, and trying to align various parts of the overall strategy.

3. Ways in which you can generate revenue from your events

The most obvious way to generate revenue is to charge individuals for attending the events. And there is a right time to do that. But as already noted, charging for events will reduce attendance growth. So let's explore some ways you can generate revenue by keeping your events free.

One common thing you can try to do is to have sponsors. Sponsors come in a few shapes and sizes. You can have sponsors who will directly give you cash to promote something of theirs, or provide a venue for your events, or provide something free to give away during your events in a contest or a raffle drawing.

Of course, since we are now focusing on generating revenue, we care about sponsors that contribute cash. Keep in mind that sponsors typically want to reach a significant number of people. So the sooner you build a big list of attendees and get their email addresses, or regularly have very high attendance, the sooner sponsors will flock to your events. But keep in mind that trying to get sponsors too early might be a waste of time because if you don't have many people to promote the events to, sponsors won't be too interested.

Over time, if you do noteworthy things and get some publicity, sponsors will begin reaching out to you. But that is only over time, if you are *consistent* and eventually successful.

When I ran my own event series, of course, I made the mistake of trying to get sponsors too early. All that resulted in was some conversations that eventually resulted in a NO, and wasted my time. But as my events grew, I was able to have more fruitful and successful conversations with different sponsors and partners for my events. Once different companies saw that I was able to get their products in front of many people who fit their ideal customer profiles, they were all too eager to send me free samples of their products (which you can keep or use as raffle prizes) or cash in exchange for promotion.

Another way you can generate revenue at your events is by selling food or products. This is especially good if you have a longer event because people will get hungry, and you can sell them food directly, or get a vendor to pay you to be present at your event and sell food there.

In my case, since I ran outdoor events, I would come to my hiking events with a car full of things like sunscreen, hats, water and light snacks, and just let people know that these are available for purchase if they forgot it at home. And, of course, many people did forget those items at home, and ended up buying them from me.

It wasn't a lot of money and truthfully, there was some awkwardness in announcing that I have things for sale right at the beginning of the event before the attendees got any value from the event, but at times when I did this, it put an extra bit of revenue directly in my pocket, which was certainly welcome, and it didn't hurt attendance.

Once you have sponsors, it is also a great way to give them a plug by giving away something free of theirs at the beginning of the event that the attendees might find useful and appreciate. Just a word of warning: don't give away any old thing. Make sure that it actually does make the lives of your attendees better.

Another very interesting thing you can try to do to generate revenue from free events is to ask for donations, or ask people to pay whatever price they choose. What that does is it allows you to keep your events listed as free and to generate maximum attendance. At the same time, if people enjoy the event, and you ask for donations in a professional, polite but assertive way, you will be surprised by how many people will give you donations.

You might also be pleasantly surprised by the size of a few of those donations which might be higher than what you expected. But that would happen only if the people truly loved and enjoyed your events. So don't forget about that leg of the 3-legged stool which is your event quality.

Keep in mind that not everyone will donate or pay if given a choice. But because you maximized attendance by making it free, giving people the option to donate and choose the amount will balance out the people who come for free.

Using this strategy, you can get a surprisingly similar number of attendees who give you donations as you would if you just charged for attendance upfront, but limited the total number of attendees.

Another way to make money from your events is to sell them branded products like t-shirts, hats or anything that will be useful to them, and have your logo and maybe website (that could be a bit too much) printed on those products. This way you can generate extra revenue while turning people into, as I endearingly call them, walking advertisements for your business.

And by the way, you yourself should be a walking advertisement for your business by having a branded shirt and maybe even a hat during your events. I'll touch more on this in a later section of the chapter.

If your events take only a few hours, and not more than a full day, what you can do is up-sell longer, maybe full-weekend seminars or getaways for which you can charge hundreds or even thousands of dollars per person. This isn't easy to do when you start, but once you've grown a bit, and people recognize and trust your brand, or you have some loyal attendees who attend regularly, you can pitch the bigger full-day or multi-day events to your most loyal and engaged attendees because in those longer events they would ideally get much more value and enjoyment.

Another strategy you can employ to generate revenue from your events is to up-sell some of your professional or consulting services, or some high-end products of yours if you have a business that sells any products or services.

Another thing some people do is use an event series to make themselves "an authority" in their business niche. Having a big event series of which you are the organizer makes you a visible and popular person in your industry. As a result of that, many people will want to work with you and network with you because you have a significant asset (your events) that you own, out of which can come multiple benefits for people.

Being such an authority or "mover and shaker" in your industry or business niche can get you jobs or consulting contracts that will pay you much more than you would typically get paid at similar jobs if you didn't have your event series.

And very often in the cases of such jobs or consulting projects, they only become available to you as a result of having a big event series and a large marketing reach. So you can make pretty significant money from your events in an indirect way like this.

There are many indirect benefits for becoming an authority or a known person/brand in your industry. People will begin to want to be associated with you and want to network with you. That will result in more publicity for you and your business, more favors for you and your business, and that publicity and favors is something I will touch more on in later sections of this chapter, especially when discussing marketing and promotion for your events.

In the case of my own event series, once I started generating publicity for my events (and I will teach you how to do that for your events and your local business shortly), those publicity pieces came in the form of articles which linked to my website. And that helped my SEO (search engine optimization) which propelled my website up in Google search rankings and drove much more attendance to my events and clients to my business. So look forward to my tips on how to do that, a little later in this book when I discuss the marketing for your events.

Also, something to really keep and mind and something that I will also cover in the section on marketing your events is the idea of identifying people who are willing to pay and spend money, and getting them to spend money again and again. Every business or event series has a top 5% or 10% of people who come in contact with it, and love that business so much that they become regular customers and spend a disproportionate amount more money than everyone else.

You must identify who those people are, treat them extra well, and offer additional products specifically to them or with them in mind. These are the types of people who might be interested in your multi-day events whereas other people who casually attend won't really be ready to buy premium products.

And before I move on, let me list a couple of additional benefits of making your events free. First, if there is another event series out there with similar events to yours, and they charge money to attend, you can suffocate their attendance by making yours free, and drawing many of their attendees to leave their events and attend yours.

Another benefit of having a free event is that you can get the free attendees who appreciate that your events are free to promote your events on their social media accounts, and to invite their friends. This will give you an even faster rate of growth for your event series. And ironically, if people bring friends, due to peer pressure and not wanting to seem like a jerk in front of their friends, they will give more and bigger donations when you ask for those donations (or ask people to choose whatever price they want to pay for the event).

This is actually what happened in my events. Whenever I asked people to donate, consistently the biggest donors were couples. The guys used to give bigger than average donations because they felt the scrutiny and pressure by their dates, and didn't want to appear cheap.

4. How to choose a price for your events if you do charge for attendance

As you just read, there are many options for you to make money from events without having to charge for attendance directly. But there may be a point when you are ready to set a price for your event. So let's cover how to choose the ideal price for your event series.

In general pricing theory, it is widely agreed that going up in price is easier than going down. What that means for you is that starting at a relatively low price points is a fine thing to do because you can go up in price from there. And gradually going up in price lets you test how many people attend at different price points so that over time you can identify an ideal price point which generates maximum revenue for your events.

Plus, having a cheaper price gives you an extra marketing weapon/angle because you can tell people that your future events will be more expensive and they "should take advantage of current low prices."

Does that phrase sound familiar? Using low price discounts and promotions is a widely used tactic in advertisements and promotions. You hear this in just about every commercial break on TV, especially in car commercials where they throw in phrases like "while supplies last" which creates a feeling of scarcity and gets people to rush to buy the product! So if creating scarcity works for those other businesses, it can work for you if you tell people that this low price offer is only available for a limited time, and only for this event (or some time period) and will go up soon.

Long-term, whatever prices you choose, you can entice people to attend by offering them discounts. What discounts do is kind of shock people with a high price, and then give them a lower price. After the shock of the higher price, the lower price seems much better. Plus, it lets you raise prices while still allowing to keep the price low for some people.

You can also use discounts to create urgency. For example, if the event is one month away, you can give a 50% discount to people who buy tickets a month in advance, and only a 25% discount to people who buy 1 week in advance and a 10% discount to people who buy 3 days in advance. People will jump on the cheaper discounted offer and start swelling your attendance number.

For most events, a majority of people decide on whether they will attend in the last few days. And if they see that the event already has so many registrants a month or a week in advance, it will make it appear as though the event is even more special and unique than what they thought it would be, and that would get people to decide to come at the last minute, and pay premium prices.

As your events grow and you start to have trouble meeting demand and selling the events out, that will be a good time to begin either raising prices or getting a larger venue. The more you raise prices, the more you decrease attendance. But the quality of each attendee who pays a higher price is higher.

Since they are willing to pay higher prices, the attendees will have more natural interest in the content of the events, and will be more likely to spend money on other things you try to sell to them. So raising prices (while providing great value) is a great way to reach higher-end clients.

Many businesses really covet higher end clients because those people can spend more money. But I want to give you some food for thought on that point. Walmart is more profitable than any high end designer brand. If you can get many people to pay a lower price and just get a bigger space for your event, it might be more lucrative than having fewer high-end clients pay higher prices.

But take all that with a grain of salt. Since there are so many kinds of events out there, I can't know what price or client discount strategy would work best for your unique situation. What you must do is experiment and calibrate. Also, talk to your event attendees, and get their thoughts on the pricing, and other aspects of your events. Especially ask them how to improve your events. They will surely have many opinions how you can do better. You don't necessarily have to take all of their advice, especially since the advice will often be directly conflicting, but you can always give it some thought, and use it to inform whatever decisions you will make in the future.

Quick note on charging for events or charging for anything else: many first-time entrepreneurs have a hard time charging for something. I am not saying that this is necessarily the case for you, but it is likely that if this is your first business, you may feel some apprehension about charging for events. I know that this was the case for me when I started. Asking people for money can be awkward. And I probably maximized the awkwardness of it because I recall feeling very uneasy about charging people money.

I would advise to take that leap and charge at least a small fee. If you are really apprehensive about charging, maybe keep the events free until you are certain that people are getting great value from the events. That knowledge will make you more confident when charging.

Plus, your efforts and your time are worth you getting paid. And if your attendees see your low confidence in your pricing strategy, they will read into it that the event really isn't worth the price. After all, if even the event organizer doesn't appear confident in their pricing or asking people to pay, how can the attendees be expected to feel good about paying? So try to be confident about your event quality and about your time being worth getting paid for.

5. Hiring staff for your event

If your event series grows to be big enough, you will need to hire some staff. So let me explain how to get staff for free or at a very affordable rate.

As soon as you start charging for attendance, you will get some people asking you for a favor to give them free access. These people will probably never pay anyway. So what you can do is give them free access in exchange for doing some job at the event. This is a simple way to get some free labor and make some friends because those people will most likely appreciate that you gave them free entrance to your paid event.

If you can't get enough free labor, you can get very cheap (or is the politically correct term "affordable" labor?) on local concierge websites. A couple of such popular websites are fancyhands.com and taskrabbit.com - there you can find people who will do odd jobs, and you can hire them for a day to help out with your event.

Just a quick note on these kinds of sites, in different countries and cities, different such sites are popular. So wherever you live, the website examples I gave may or may not be the most popular sites. What I recommend that you do is first check out those websites, but if you don't find any great help there, just search Google for something like "hire someone for one day in your_city_name" where your_city_name is the name of your actual city. Or try a variety of similar searches until you find a good website for this sort of thing for your local area.

In United States, for a full day's work, these people will often charge only $100 or possibly less. So you get good value from them. And for just a few hours worth of work you can maybe get away with paying under $50 or even $30.

If you charge for events, and these laborers will help to improve the quality of the event, and help you make the event run more smoothly, it will help to get more people to enjoy the events, and to recommend your future events to their friends, and themselves attend more of your events.

Additionally, the more people enjoy your events, the more likely they will be to engage with whatever products or services you try to sell them. So hiring help can seem like a waste of money, but if the people you hire help to make the events better, it can help to generate revenue for you to more than compensate for the help you hired.

Another way to get free labor at your events is to ask friends and family to help out. Not everyone will be excited to help you, but some friends and family might actually be eager to help you and to see you succeed. So a few people might jump at the opportunity to help you. It will be a nice way to do something together with them while getting free labor for your events.

One caveat, of course, is that it is often risky to mix friends, family and business. Some disagreements may lead to harming your relationships with your friends and family. So you should think twice before inviting your friends and family to help at your events because you certainly don't want to risk harming the relationships you have with them.

Another point on growing your events and hiring staff is that as early as possible in the lifetime of your events, you should focus on branding. This means that all event staff, including yourself, should wear company-branded clothing. The clothing that you choose should be appropriate for the type of event you have.

The more people are bombarded with your logo and your business name, and your event name, the more likely they will remember all those things and come back to attend future events.

Let me tell you about a revelation I once had when I was running my own events. It was a hike event, and I was walking and chatting with one of the hikers. The conversation turned to my own events and my website. Now mind you that I had gotten the URL for my website to be so simple that people could never confuse it or misspell it or forget it. The URL is comehike.com which is two very simple English words that make sense together and are almost impossible to misspell. That's what I thought anyway. That assumption quickly dissipated after the hiker with whom I was chatting said something like "what was your website name? Is it GoHike.com or GoHiking.com or LetsHike?"

This is when I realized that I can't rely on people to remember my business or website name no matter how simple or memorable the business name might seem to me.

What does that mean for you? You need to focus on your branding so that your attendees see your business name and website name many times throughout the event, and get used to it. Each extra time they see your business name, event brand, or website URL, it will increase the likelihood of them being able to remember it, re-connect online, attend more of your events, build more of a relationship with your business and event series, and hopefully eventually buy whatever you try to sell.

For that reason, having branded uniforms is extra important. So I would urge you to give it some priority. Plus, even though I don't run the hiking events anymore, I still have some of the t-shirts from those events that I sometimes wear, and it is nice to have them because they bring back all the fun memories I had running those events.

Plus, having branded uniforms will help the attendees know who the staff is and who can help them if they are confused with anything.

Now let's talk about how to hire the actual individuals after you find them online and after you have the uniforms for them. No matter how good their online reviews might be or what nice things they say about themselves, you should always meet them before the event. You don't need to meet them for a long time. Often, just a 10-15 minute conversation can help you understand whether they are appropriate for your event. You won't always be correct in that judgement that you get to form within 10-15 minutes, but you will certainly be able to weed out some of the very low quality people.

And that is what you really want to do: avoid hiring the bottom 25%. Hiring bad staff can turn your attendees off from your events, waste a lot of your time, some of your money, and discourage your other employees and lower overall morale. And if you can't have a person to person meeting with potential hires, at least take the time to talk to them on the phone to see how they communicate, how pleasant they might be, and get a feel for other things that they do or do not bring to the table.

Once you do add staff members, make sure that you welcome them and make them feel like an important part of the team by giving them specific responsibilities. Whenever people know what their jobs are, and what is expected of them, they make sure to do that. Even if they turn out to be slackers, most of the time they will still do the bare minimum main responsibility that you give them.

Overall, for all your staff, do try to make them feel like each of their unique tasks is very important and that they have a lot of responsibility. Make them feel respected, and keep an open door policy for them to be able to reach out to you and talk to you about anything at almost any time. Sometimes they won't like the job, but out of appreciation and respect for you, they will be motivated to do it better. And take the time to greet all your staff and thank them for their unique contributions. They will appreciate it.

Pro tip: when you thank anyone, don't just give them a plain thank you. It is really impersonal, and simply saying "thank you" that you easily give just about everyone else doesn't show a whole lot of appreciation. After all, how much effort did it take you to quickly say thanks and forget the person?

Instead of giving a simple thanks, tell them thank you for whatever good thing they did. For example, "thank you for managing attendance so carefully" or "thank you for being so proactive to help people find their seats" or other similar ways to express your gratitude. Thanking for specific things gets much more appreciation from whoever you are thanking.

6. Do you need to register your event as a business entity?

This is a legal discussion. And I am not a lawyer. So I must add the disclaimer that for true legal advice you should contact a lawyer or at least some legal professional who can be more authoritative and credible on the subject.

Full disclaimer: I do not give any legal advice anywhere in this book.

Disclaimer two: The issues I will discuss here apply to United States law only. If you are in a different country, please research what laws apply to your unique situation wherever you are located.

I did make a full online course on small business law with my lawyer. You can check out how to get it for free at the very end of the book where I discuss the free gifts I offer to readers of this book, and some of the very affordable additional resources and help.

But let's return to the main subject matter of this chapter. Here I'll just give you a few basic things to keep in mind when it comes to understanding whether you need to register your events as a business, or run the events under your main business or "as self" which is what happens when you don't have a business entity.

One of the biggest benefits of registering a business entity and running your events under that business entity is that you get limited liability protection. That means that if someone sues you, and wins, they don't sue you for your personal assets like your money, house, car, furniture or clothing. All they do is sue the business. But if you don't open a company and don't run your events under that company, if someone sues you and wins, they will be suing you for your actual personal possessions and the money in your bank account, your car, your house and so on. You can potentially stand to lose everything you personally own.

So registering a business entity and running your main business and your events under that business can help you decrease the risk of losing your and your family's house, possessions and savings.

In United States, you register a business by going through your state's Secretary Of State Office. Every state has a Secretary Of State Office, and you can contact your state's office online or on the phone, and they will explain to you the steps you need to go through in order to register your business entity.

There is also some consideration of what kind of a business entity to open. It will also have tax implications. But since I am neither an accountant or a lawyer, and not truly qualified to advise on those issues, I will defer you to get help from those professionals on these issues. I would also encourage you to explore the online business law course which I mentioned that I made with my lawyer. In that course he explains how you can decide what kind of a business entity is right for you.

7. Do you need to get insurance for your event?

The reasoning of whether to buy insurance for your event series is somewhat similar to the reasoning for whether you should register a business entity to get limited liability protection. It also depends on the kind of events you run.

If your events are something where people have a higher chance of having accidents or getting injured, then it begins to make more sense to buy insurance for your events. Similarly, if your events become very large, and people start seeing you as a bag of money, they might be more likely to make some claim of damages for one reason or another. And having insurance gives you a little more peace of mind.

But at the end of the day, insurance isn't free. It is a cost. And you must evaluate it as any other cost that you might incur in your business, and decide whether it is worth getting insurance for your business.

8. Getting an event venue

In this section of the chapter, I'll explain how to find a free or cheap event venue for your event series.

Having a venue means an increased cost for your business. The cost isn't just financial. The cost is also your time and effort in doing appropriate research and due diligence, contacting different venues, talking to the managers there, scheduling (and re-scheduling) things, and many more organizational details, all of which take up your time which significantly adds to the overall expense of getting a venue.

Since actual venues have a financial cost to them, at first consider what free options you have. The most common free option to run your events outside. While this is obviously not a possibility for all types of events, it works great for exercise groups. If the weather is nice, it can work well for some hobby or interest groups. In fact, doing an event outside can give you extra marketing because random people outside might see your big and fun gathering and might inquire about your events, and eventually might become attendees themselves.

Even if the kinds of events you put on don't immediately seem like they can be put on outside, give it some thought. You might come up with some creative and even fun solution that could make it more enjoyable for your attendees, save you money on not needing a venue, and might even give you a unique marketing angle if you do figure out something creative for how you will run your event outside.

The second option you have to get a free venue is to put on your events in coffee shops, restaurants or bars. Those kinds of venues really like it when you bring them people during off-peak hours. During peak hours they are usually overfilled, but in off-peak hours they are often empty. And if you can bring 10-20 (or however many) people to their businesses during off-peak hours, they might offer some extra group discounts, and welcome the potential customers that you will bring them.

The problem with coffee shops, restaurants or bars is that usually most events happen during weekends or evenings, which is their peak hours because that is when most people are off from work. So it isn't actually easy to bring them many people in non-peak hours, and it still leaves the problem of finding a venue for peak hours.

The next strategy to get a free venue is to find companies that have office spaces. These companies should target the same types of people that your events tend to attract. This way, if the events are in the evenings or weekends, most of the company staff is out of the office, and the meeting rooms become available. They often welcome events there because it means extra awareness and promotion to those businesses to your attendees, some of whom might get interested in the products and services of that business.

So you must network and reach out to managers at companies which target the same sort of customers as your event series draws, and you might work out a deal to get free space to run your events in exchange for a little bit of extra promotion for that business.

You may also consider running the event at your company's physical location if that is possible for the kind of space that you have. This can bring people right to your business, which is obviously great for you.

At some point, when you generate significant demand for your events, you will outgrow these types of mid-side event spaces. Congratulations if you are at that point!

If you begin to need bigger spaces, you can rent space in hotels. They often have "ballrooms" which they rent out to different events. And once you outgrow that, you can rent out full events spaces.

But generally, over 90% of the kinds of events that might be run by individuals or small businesses never need hotel ballrooms or large event or conference spaces. So if you are resourceful and creative, you should be able to get free (or extremely discounted) event spaces as your events grow.

9. Prizes and raffles to make your event more fun and attractive

Some event organizers like to give away prizes or raffles at their events. It makes the events more fun, memorable, and adventurous for your attendees.

The challenge with giving things away is that you are losing money by giving things away. So ideally, you would give things away from sponsors whom you can promote while announcing the raffle and then again when announcing the winner of the raffle.

Sponsors do tend to take a long time to get on board. So if you want to have raffles and prizes at your events, you must do two things:

1) Get on their radar early and start a conversation with them about potentially sponsoring the events. It will take time for their internal company discussions and any business development matter to get resolved. So the sooner you start pursuing this, the sooner it will happen for you. Don't only focus on this in the last minute.

2) Don't try to get sponsors too early. Sponsors want to reach many highly targeted people. So if you don't have too great of an attendance at your events just yet, first focus on growing your event series, and once you have the people, the sponsors will come.

EVENT MARKETING AND GENERATING AMAZING ATTENDANCE

Let's explore what's to come in this marketing section. I will explain to you how to use scalable online marketing strategies, leverage SEO (search engine optimization), your website and other online websites to draw people to your events, and then to make your attendees long-term attendees and clients of your other products and services. I will also explain how to get your events to really stand out, and generate publicity and extra attention for you, your events, and ultimately your main business which you are trying to promote with the events.

These strategies worked like a charm for me. But it does take attention to detail from you, and a serious effort from you. So please follow the suggestions carefully.

Additionally, some of the topics like SEO are pretty gigantic topics to cover in enough detail in this book, the focus of which is events and not SEO. For topics like that, at the end of the book I will have a way for you to get free and affordable online courses on topics like SEO and many more additional resources, or my one-on-one coaching to help you create a really good marketing strategy for your event series.

10. Collecting contact information and building regular attendance

Do you ever hear people mention how email marketing is gold, and that this is where they truly make their money? Do you wonder how or why it is specifically email marketing?

I will tell you. The secret is in the fact that people almost never change email addresses, and it is a relatively intimate place to reach them. If people open your emails, chances are that they will read your email. And if your emails regularly bring them great value, interest or entertainment, they will engage with your mailings more and more.

Precisely this intimate re-engagement and your ability to reach people time and time again is why email marketing can be so much more effective than other promotional methods at generating clients and increasing engagement.

This section goes a little bit beyond email in suggesting that you collect any kind of contact information in an effort to be able to broadcast future announcements to your audience as much as possible.

In addition to collecting email addresses, try to get people to follow you on Twitter, or like your page or group on Facebook or connect with you on LinkedIn. The goal isn't for you to get more likes. The goal is to be able to re-engage those people in the future in as many ways as possible in the future when you need to promote new events or anything else to them.

What is the common thread here? In all these cases you will have a way to reach those people when you announce your upcoming events **and** all those platforms also make it relatively easy to get those people to forward the information about your events or product promotions to their friends, and invite their friends to come to your events or take advantage of sales and product promotions that your business has in the future.

Of all those social platforms, on average, getting people's email addresses and marketing future events or sales to them via email is by far much more effective than Twitter, Facebook or other social sites. So while the most coveted piece of contact information to collect is an email address, redundancy in having multiple points of contact is even more ideal. So if you can, get people's email addresses AND Twitter AND get them to engage on Facebook, LinkedIn or wherever else your event series and business has a presence. It becomes that much more effective since on average they will get more reminders about your future events and other kinds of announcements.

Ideally you want to build long-term fans. The more people will attend your events, the more they will spend directly on attendance fees, and the more likely they will be to engage with any other products or services that you try to sell them in the future. That makes having a way to remind them of upcoming events or any other future promotions absolutely crucial.

For any business, a large part of the marketing focus should be on retaining existing customers because as a rule of thumb, it is easier to sell to an existing customer than to sell to a new customer. And since existing customers already trust you more, they may also spend higher amounts of money.

Here are the ideal times when to try collecting email addresses and contact information:

- When people sign up for your events online
- When people register at the event as they arrive to the place of the event and you check them off the attendance list to make sure they arrived
- When you run raffles and prize giveaways, collect business cards
- Always remind people to follow you on Twitter and like your page or join your group on Facebook. You will be able to promote your future events and business announcements there to them.
- During the event, if possible, have a highly visible spot where you keep the URLs to your Twitter or Facebook pages, and your website.

- During the event, take a moment to remind your attendees to follow, like, or subscribe to your email newsletter to get notified when you schedule upcoming events.

And most importantly, one of the biggest factors in helping you get repeat attendance is the event quality itself. Do what you can to put on events that are as best as reasonably possible. The more people like your events, the more they will naturally come back, and your email reminders will be a welcome thing to them.

The big point to ponder and focus on: everything you do should have a focus on retaining your customers long-term and get regular attendees for multiple events. This is why I emphasized this point as the very first thing I wanted to cover in the marketing section. If you can get someone to attend many of your events and engage in additional things you sell, you can earn thousands of percent more revenue from them compared to what they would spend if they only attended one of your events.

11. Attracting attendance

Let me tell you how attendance grew at my own events. At first, almost no one attended outdoor events or hikes that I organized. I would get very few sign-ups on my website, come to the event meeting point and have zero or one or two people join, and we would go on a hike together. I still had to put on a happy face, but inside I was very sad and disappointed because my events were struggling, and I wasn't solving the poor attendance issue. As an event organizer, having no attendance is just about the worst and most frustrating thing that can happen to you, and in the beginning, this is exactly what was happening to me. It was giving me a very dejected and empty feeling, and I was very discouraged about my entire business and event idea, and often thought about stopping the whole thing, calling it a failure, and moving on with my life.

Then one day I got advice from a very experienced business person whom I had the luck to meet at a networking event. I only had 2 minutes of conversation with him, but he advised me to try to get a lot of publicity and attention by doing some very risky or even illegal outdoor events or hikes.

At first, that advice was very disappointing to me. I didn't want to do anything illegal, nor did I know how to create such an event. But I started to give this sort of a concept some thought. And a few weeks later an idea hit me which would eventually pave the way to my success.

Let me tell you about this idea. At that time I was living in San Francisco, California. If you are not familiar with the geography of San Francisco, it is almost an island, and surrounded by water on three sides. There is a large and rocky coastline. And I learned that decades ago, before ships had good navigation systems, many ships would crash on the rocky coastline and sink. I also learned that during low tide, some of those shipwrecks were visible.

That was my AHA! moment. I was going to organize a hike during low tide to catch a glimpse of the shipwrecks! I was very excited (partially because I am such a nerd, and myself wanted to see the shipwrecks more than anyone). I posted this event on my website, and a couple of other websites, and waited for an increased number of attendees.

I waited and waited...and waited, and people still weren't signing up on my website. So I thought that it was going to be another dud event. But like always, despite already preparing myself for disappointment, I came to the event meeting place about 15 minutes early as the punctual event organizer that I am.

But something was different about it this time.

Right where I planned my own event, stood a group of about 50 people who I didn't know. I thought "wow, that's just great. Not only will I have almost no attendees, but the few attendees that will come to my event will get confused by this large group of people." I was double disappointed and frustrated.

But then a funny thing happened. I asked those people what they were waiting there for, and they said they were there for a shipwreck hike that someone by the name of Alex Genadinik (that is me!!) organized.

I was floored! 50 people who came 15 minutes before the event! How? Why? What happened? These were all questions that raced through my mind.

I didn't have time to look for an answer to these questions because someone quickly pointed out to me that there was another group of about 40-50 people standing half a block away.

In a very confused, anxious, but excited. In that state I walked over to that group and asked them why they were there, and they too, told me that they were there for my event.

I invited them to join the original group, and as things got closer to the start time of the event people kept on rapidly arriving and swelling the numbers of my attendees. Many of them were bringing their kids to see the shipwrecks, their dogs and many friends.

People kept coming until about 15 minutes past when the event was supposed to start, and I had easily 200-300 people on my hands. People were still arriving, but the now hundreds of people in attendance pressured me to get started with the event so I did.

I had absolutely no idea how to handle this number of people. We were supposed to go on a hike, and walk on a trail that is at most 2-people wide. And there was only one of me. If I led the hike, how would I know what is happening at the end of the hike? If I walked in the middle of the group or in the back, the people in the front would have no idea where to go. In short, it was insane.

I completely mismanaged the hike, but I could not be more excited about the number of attendees that finally came to my event after all that effort and frustration. After regularly having less than 5 people join my hikes, this was such a happy relief.

You may be wondering how I got such large attendance all of a sudden. I'll tell you. Because the headline of my event was so exciting (it was: "Shipwreck hunt during low tide in San Francisco"), it turned out to easily be the most exciting event in the city that day. The event was incredibly unique. So the Sunday paper for the entire city of San Francisco ended up noticing it, and publishing a **front-page ad** about my shipwreck hike.

Do you remember A of AIDA? The A stands for attention, and you often grab attention with your headlines. That certainly worked like a charm here.

The big impact: The event title was so attractive, flashy and grabbed so much immediate attention that it literally drew the curiosity of local press, and got me publicity.

So guess what I did? Every week after that, I ran a new very flashy themed event. I added a hike through a military base, seasonal nature hikes, even geeky hikes to the statue of Yoda (for Stars Wars fans), scavenger hikes, and wine tasting hikes. And, of course, my biggest draw was the shipwreck hike which I made into a recurring, monthly event.

Not all the hike themes were a hit, but most were! All those flashy, attention-grabbing themes got me quite a bit of publicity.

In the next sections I will explain to you how exactly I leveraged that publicity to grow the events and my overall business even more.

12. Local event websites

Let me explain to you how a lot of the publicity even had a chance to happen in the first place. You might be asking yourself how the local newspaper found out about my shipwreck hike in the first place.

I'll tell you how, and the beauty of it is that you can easily reproduce that I did.

In whatever city you live, there are many local-event websites. Even if you live in a tiny town, the big city nearby has many websites that focus on local events. For every city, those websites are different so I can't tell you which one will work in your city. But I can tell you how to find them.

To find such websites for the big city that is most relevant for where you run your events, just search google for something like "your event type in city name" which in my case was "hiking in San Francisco" or "outdoor events San Francisco" and you will get many results. Or you can even search something more basic like "events in city_name" where city_name is the name of your city, to find all the sites that list events for your local area.

Some of those search results will be from event-listing websites where you can add your events! Those kinds of sites are referred to as user generated content websites where the users (you) can post content (your events).

Go through the first 50 listings of the search results or so to make completely certain that you don't miss any such sites that might not immediately show up on the first page. In my case, I identified about 7 very good websites where I promoted every one of my events. It is on one of those websites that the local newspaper discovered my shipwreck hike, which resulted in all that extra publicity.

And the best thing is that if you post events there consistently (remember the idea of doing the events consistently that I mentioned in the beginning of the book?) the editors of those sites will begin to recognize your events, and give you extra promotion.

That is what happened in my case. Over time, I developed relationships with editors or owners of those event listing websites, and they gave me extra promotion every week because they knew that people loved my events and that I took the extra care and effort to make the events great and attractive.

This gave me a reliable weekly way to get great attendance to my events. And it was completely free. This is something you can easily reproduce on your own, wherever you might be located.

If you don't mind paying a few bucks, there are a couple of very affordable paid options which can give you an even bigger boost in attendance. I'll mention two such strategies here.

1) Meetup.com is a great website on which you can organize your own event group, and post your events. There are millions of people using Meetup.com worldwide and it is the single biggest events website in the world. It isn't free, but it is very affordable. And if you can generate revenue from your events, the attendees that it will bring to your events will pay for the Meetup.com fees many times over. If I was starting a new event series today, it would be a an almost automatic choice for me to try to leverage meetup.com as best I possibly can. Meetup.com doesn't have to be (and shouldn't be) your only source for event promotion, but it is a great one to add to your list of promotion options.

Full disclaimer: I am **NOT** affiliated with meetup.com in any way

2) The other strategy you can try to use is the "promoted event" option that most local event websites offer. Usually the

way these kinds of event listing websites work is they allow you to post your event listings for free. But if you pay them some fee like $19.99 or $29.99 or whatever they may charge (usually pretty affordable), they can give you a boosted premium listing which is sure to draw many more attendees to your events. And again, if you have a way to make money from your events, the revenue that you will generate from doing this should pay for the promoted listing fee and then some.

13. Your website

In addition to posting your events on large local-event websites, you can also post your events on your company's website.

Many people struggle with creating their own websites because it often takes a long time, and is expensive if you have to hire someone to create the website for you.

But luckily, there is Wordpress which allows you to create a great website on your own, for just about free, in a relatively short time. Wordpress now powers about 20% of all websites online, and is an industry standard for many types of businesses.

To help you create your own website without having to hire anyone, I created two online courses that can fully guide you through the process:

1) How to find a great domain name for your business
2) How to create a Wordpress website in as little as 1 day (or just a few days)

Discounts and ways to get the courses for *free* can be found in the very end of this book in the section with further resources.

So now you will be able to easily create your own website in just a few days, and all of a sudden more marketing options open up to you. You can now publish the event announcements on your website, and your website can rank in Google search for searches like "event type in city_name." For example, the important searches in my case were "group hikes in San Francisco" or "outdoor groups in San Francisco."

On your website you can also give people the option to sign up for your email updates and to follow you on your social media accounts. And that will allow you to reach people when you announce your future events, and turn people into regular attendees.

14. SEO (search engine optimization) for your website

SEO is a huge topic, and again, since it is outside the scope of event planning, I have a full course on this that will make you an SEO expert and help you understand how to make your website and pages rank well in Google searches.

I apologize for constantly mentioning the courses, but they are truly helpful, and get you up and running very quickly. Plus, since this is a local business marketing book, many of the subjects around which I mention my courses (like building a website or SEO) don't fit into the scope of this book. So the courses are a fantastic resource for you to use.

Now that I explained myself, and why I keep alluding to the courses, let me explain why SEO is so important and after that I'll do my best to cover the basics of SEO that are relevant for your event marketing.

Imagine if you walk up to a random person and tell them to sign up for anything or buy something. In most cases they would just ignore you because either your offer or the timing of your offer isn't right for them. But when people search for something in Google, the timing and what they are searching for is exactly right for them right there and then. So a website visitor from Google search is typically much more engaged than some random person who might find you elsewhere.

Now that you understand why SEO traffic from Google is so valuable, let me explain some of the points of how this pertains to our event marketing.

Even though SEO is very complex, and I do strongly urge you to go through my online course on it, I can significantly simplify it here for you by tying many other parts of the strategy together.

First, I want to quickly go over the two most important concepts in SEO:

1) Choosing the kinds of keywords that you want your website to rank for is crucial. If I have hiking events, and people somehow discover me through searching "running in San Francisco" they will just click away because my site isn't relevant for them. But if the website ranks in Google for the exactly correct keywords that are relevant for the actual content of your website, the traffic will really engage with your website.

2) After you choose the correct keywords to rank for, you must actually begin to rank for those keywords in Google searches. And while there are many factors that go into getting your website to rank highly in Google searches, the single biggest ranking factor is the relevance, quality, authority, and quantity of the links that point to your website from other sites on the web.

Consider the second point, and now let me explain how the strategy comes full circle.

Remember how earlier in this chapter I explained how to get publicity and how to post your events on all kinds of different local event websites? Well, guess what? All those publicity and event-listing mentions usually have a link pointing from their websites to yours!!! Yes that deserved 3 exclamation marks!

Pursuing the strategy of getting publicity and getting links from other sites will boost you in Google search rankings, and over time, you will be getting lots of traffic and attendance from Google search because due to all those links pointing to your website, your website will rank highly in Google searches and draw a significant amount of traffic! Isn't that amazing? This is what happened in my events business, and this is precisely what fueled a very large part of the growth of that business and my overall event series.

Let me actually tell you what happened in my business. After my website got publicity many times and was featured and linked to by many other websites, it started being very authoritative in Google search, and achieved very high Google search rankings. After I saw that, I started adding many new web-pages to the website, with each page targeting some new relevant search term to rank for. And most of the pages were ranking quite well, and bringing me more and more traffic.

This was essentially the key to the success of that business. I was able to grow search traffic, event attendance and revenue from publicity, social media sharing from my attendees, and from getting new attendees who discovered my events via Google search. I grew that business until I started my current business which helps entrepreneurs.

Over time, I moved from San Francisco and there was no one to run the events business, and it slowly declined, and now the website is just a shell of its former self.

But if I had wanted to, I could have stayed with that nice and lucrative San Francisco outdoors events business.

But don't feel sorry for me. I now have a great business that I love, which allows me to help other entrepreneurs like yourself, and it is truly my passion to help other entrepreneurs who might be just starting out so that you don't make the same mistakes that I did, and have an easier time finding success with your business than I did.

15. Branding

I already touched on branding earlier in the book. Here, I want to add just a few points on it.

First of all, one of the biggest and most memorable parts of your brand is the quality of the actual events and the quality of the products or services of your overall business. If people have a great time, you will have a great and loved brand. But if people have a boring or unsatisfactory time, that is also how your brand will be remembered.

And since your brand is ultimately the overall impression people have of your business, every point of contact they make with your event series from learning about, to registering for the events, to attending, has to be as high quality as possible.

That's all I wanted to note about basic branding because truthfully, I am much more excited about the next section which explains how to put your branding on steroids!

16. Branding on steroids

What I call branding on steroids, others sometimes call becoming a celebrity in your business niche. At first, this might sound a little funny, but bare with me. I'll explain the reasoning behind this, and hopefully you will see the awesome power of this strategy.

When I say celebrity, I don't mean like Kim Kardashian or Justin Beiber. What I mean is a business celebrity or a known person within your business niche, a thought leader or a mover and shaker if you will.

Once you are perceived as a leader in your business niche, people will suddenly want to network with you, do you favors, and to generally associate with you. This will give you more marketing, more authority, more publicity, and more trust from your potential customers, which will result in more sales since people need to trust you before they buy from you.

So how do you actually become a celebrity? It is actually not that difficult. What you must do is create a big platform for yourself or create a big product. Let me explain what I mean.

Think of any business celebrity. How did they get to be very well known in their industry? They either wrote a very successful book, had a very big YouTube or podcast show, or built a big company, and are now known through that. And having your own big event series can give you that big platform to stand on, and be known by. And of course, having lots of publicity that you might generate through the methods I outlined above can further help to establish you as somewhat of a celebrity in your niche.

Once you make your event series a very big and prominent one, you will be automatically seen as somewhat of a celebrity in your business niche. I am not saying that it will make you the top person in your niche, but I am saying that you will certainly be in the top 10% of the more powerful people in your niche, and many additional benefits will come from that long-term.

17. Generating publicity and standing out above the crowd

I already discussed how you can generate publicity for your business, but there is one more point I want to emphasize. It is that you should always try to stand out.

For example, recall how no one wanted to go on regular hikes with me, but hundreds of people wanted to go on a cool and exciting sounding hike.

This is what you should try to do with your event series and your business in general. Think of what creative angles you can take, or do something more flashy that will make your events more memorable, and stand out.

Recall the advice I got from the experienced business person about doing something illegal or dangerous. I am not saying that you should try to do something illegal or dangerous. But try to think of any legitimate and on-brand way to get your events to stand out. The idea for this didn't immediately come to me. It took me weeks of thinking about it. But if you mull it over long enough, it will come to you.

18. Event video, live-streaming, and YouTube promotion

Another natural and nifty way you can promote your events is if you videotape your events (if that is possible in your unique situation), and then put those videos on YouTube and *properly* promote those videos.

This way, for very little additional effort, you can begin to have a presence on YouTube, and get that massive website to drive traffic and awareness to your events.

You can also have the YouTube video transcribed, and turned into a blog post which you can then share on social media, and get to rank in Google search, which would bring you even more traffic.

CHAPTER 6: 11 OFFLINE MARKETING STRATEGIES

"Do what you can, with what you have, where you are."

- Theodore Roosevelt

1. How to get yourself appearances on the radio and podcasts

I personally have gotten over 50 podcast and radio show appearances within one year (and over 100 over time) for myself just by using this website:

http://www.radioguestlist.com

I even have an online course about how you can take the most advantage of this website here (and you can get this course as a **free** gift from me - I explain that at the end of this book):

https://www.udemy.com/how-i-got-50-podcast-appearances-using-radioguestlist/

Once you sign up for the free account on the radioguestlist.com website, every weekday they will send you a list of podcasts and radio shows which are looking for experts to interview. And you can pitch those radio show and podcast hosts to see whether they will want to interview you. You already have some pitch tools in your toolbox from chapter one, which should be a good guide for how to pitch radio stations as well.

In the online course which I mentioned that you can get for free from me, I explain and walk you through exactly how I pitched radio show and podcast hosts to get 50+ interviews for myself in just 1 year.

2. 3 ways to get business referrals

I put 3 different ways to get referrals in this section because there are many ways to get referrals, and many of them are actually not related to one another. For example, you might get a referral from an existing customer or you might get a referral from another business with whom you might have a business relationship with. These are both called referrals, but the strategies to get these referrals are pretty different. So in this section, I'll cover all the different ways to get offline referrals.

Let's start with how to get referrals from your existing customers, and get them to invite their friends. *This is also what some people sometimes refer to as word of mouth marketing.*

The most important thing when it comes to getting customer referrals is your product quality. If your product or service is amazing, and leaves your customers thrilled and feeling like they just got an amazing value, they will naturally talk about your product or services with friends, and recommend it.

But even if your customers truly love your product or service, they won't recommend it to friends that often. There just isn't enough for them in it. Remember how all your customers think and care about is what is in it for them? For that reason, you must always give them incentives, and the incentives must be for the current customer **and** any new potential customers they might bring. Let me give you an example.

If you offer a customer 20% OFF their next purchase if they bring a friend, there is not enough incentive for the friend to try out your business. And if you give 20% OFF to the friend, there is not enough incentive for the current customer to make the recommendation because there is nothing in it for the current customer. But if you give 20% OFF (or whatever other discount) to both of them, then suddenly, the current customer will have enough incentive to invite friends, and the friends will know that they will be getting a good deal, and will come more readily.

This is how you maximize your social referrals: through very high quality services and products, and double incentives. Don't just rely on people to recommend your business to others. Control, influence, and maximize it with correct incentives.

Another way to get referrals is to get professional referrals. This strategy is completely different from getting customer referrals. To get professional referrals, you need to build relationships with businesses in your industry which can refer clients to you, and you can refer clients to them.

For example, the medical community has this nailed down pat. If you go to a general physician, and he spots a skin problem, he recommends you to go to a specific skin care doctor. If you have a foot problem, he recommends a foot doctor. If he thinks some medicine can help you, he recommends that medicine. Being on that doctor's recommendation list can drive a lot of business.

This is what you have to do as well. If you are a mechanic, build relationships with companies that clean cars, paint cars, sell and install fancy rims or car stereo systems, and so on. If their customers ever have their cars break, they can refer those customers to you. And if your customers ever need a paint job or ask about car stereo systems, you can refer those people to those companies. This way you develop a professional network of companies who refer clients to one another, and boost each other's businesses.

The third way you get referrals is to pay other companies for the leads that they send you, or pay a commission after one of the leads they sent you becomes a paid customer. Paying is a very powerful way to incentivize other companies in your niche to send you leads and referrals.

3. Join a local press club

Every large city has a local press club. Outside the press world this is a little known strategy, but it can pay you amazing dividends. A press club is where journalists and press professionals meet and network.

What you can do is come to the press club events, and volunteer as an expert "source" which is the industry term for someone who contributes an expert opinion to an article. If those journalists use your expert opinion, you can get free publicity for you and your business in local newspapers, even larger publications, and sometimes even TV.

If you don't know how to find a local press club, go to Google.com and search this:
"press club in city_name" where city_name is the big city in which you live or the nearest big city to the one in which you live. Small cities don't usually have press clubs so you will have to search for the nearest big city to where you live.

Once you find your local press club, go to their website, look up the next time they meet, the requirements to attend, and then go ahead and attend that press club meeting. Come ready with your business cards, business pitch, positive body language signs and all your other strategies to get the most out of the connections you make there.

If you are in New York, for example, here is the local website for the press club:

4. Where to plaster your logo and website

Depending on the kind of business you have, different places make sense for printing your logo, business name and website URL. As a business owner, you probably wouldn't mind if the entire earth was covered with your logo. So there has to be a limit somewhere. Let's explore where it makes sense to print your logo, business name and website URL.

The first place on which you should put your logo and website URL is...YOURSELF! Get nice t-shirts and hats made that you wouldn't mind wearing. Give those t-shirts and hats to your staff as well.

If you have a local business like roofing, handyman, restaurant, or anything similar, you can also put the logo and website URL on the sides of your car, and on your bumper. If your bumper sticker is funny, it will get people's attention and stand out because typically when people are looking at your bumper, they are bored in traffic, and if you give them a little bit of extra entertainment, they will engage.

Some people also like to have pens, key-chains or other small items made with their logos on those items. I am not a fan of this strategy if your budget is tight. The only way I would pursue that strategy for a small business that is just starting out is to think about what your ideal customer does regularly, make an item that helps them with that, and put your logo/URL on that item. Then, since there is a cost to having those items made, only give that item for free to people who you think are very good potential candidates to someday become customers.

Sometimes you can charge people a few dollars to buy these items if those items are actually cool and useful. This can be nice because you get to have people pay you a little bit to advertise your company.

Since your business is a local business, you can try promoting your business or URL on a billboard if that makes financial sense for you. Typically billboards have contact information for the company who owns them, and you can call and inquire how much a billboard ad would cost, and try to negotiate a rate that would make sense for you.

5. Door to door marketing

Door to door marketing is another one of those promotional strategies that only works for some businesses and products.

Often, the kinds of products that sell well with door to door marketing are visual products that are not too expensive relative to the affluence level of the neighborhood in which you will be selling. Ideally it could be something they could use for the home. For example, I once knew of a home painter who simply walked around affluent or middle class neighborhoods and whenever he saw a home that could have used a new paint job, he would simply knock on the door and give his sales pitch. That was very effective for him, especially as he became very good at his sales pitch.

Remember your sales pitch from chapter one and the points on body language? This is where these must really work for you. If you knock on someone's door and they see that you are trying to sell them something, their initial reaction might be annoyance and irritation. In many cases you only have a few sentences to perk their interest. If you don't, they will just close the door on you.

This is why having a nicely presented visual product that might get their attention (remember A as the attention in AIDA?), and an effective sales pitch can really help make or break your sales campaign and give you a good sales conversion.

Another thing you want to try to do is to do your door to door marketing during a time of the day when the person you are selling to is at home. If you are selling something that requires the head of household's decision to buy, you want to go in the evening. And if you are selling something that requires a stay at home mom's decision to buy, you might want to go earlier in the day.

The difference between randomly trying to sell something and using a correct sales pitch with the right script with the AIDA structure in literally hundreds of percent. So make sure that your sales pitch is practiced, well scripted and works.

And keep in mind that this particular way to promote your business or products is going to have a lot of rejection. That rejection can give you low confidence. Try to catch yourself on that thought if you find yourself feeling a lack of confidence. You just have to persevere. Rejection is very much a part of sales. But if you persevere, and eventually become very good at sales, you will be able to sell anything, and it will give you a boost for the rest of your career.

6. Guerilla marketing and publicity stunts

Here is how the father of Guerrilla Marketing, Jay Conrad Levinson describes guerrilla marketing:

"I'm referring to the soul and essence of guerrilla marketing which remain as always - achieving conventional goals, such as profits and joy, with unconventional methods, such as investing energy instead of money.

To me, this means using a lot of creativity and a unique approach to promote whatever it is you are promoting. Also, to me, this is very close to Seth Godin's purple cow concept. The idea behind the concept of the Purple Cow is that since a purple cow would be something very unusual (since it doesn't exist), most people would stop to take a closer look at it if they saw one.

The idea is that you have to bring uniqueness to whatever you do, and that uniqueness will get you to stand out.

Now let me explain what publicity stunts are. They are related to guerrilla marketing. Publicity stunts are things that you specifically do to get so much attention that eventually press picks it up. To get attention you have to do something very unusual, out of the ordinary, and attention-grabbing. A classic example of this is when someone was selling people parts of the Brooklyn bridge. If you are not familiar with the Brooklyn bridge, it is a very iconic bridge, much like the Golden Gate bridge in terms of its fame.

So how can some individual be selling parts of the Brooklyn bridge? Don't they need to have permission, or to own it first? And how can they sell an entire bridge? Rumors and stories quickly spread about the person who was selling the Brooklyn bridge, and got enough attention from people to get press coverage and become such a large story that years later I am noting it here. But really, what was happening was that during regular maintenance of the bridge, little chips of the rock from the bridge would fall, and one guy would pick up those pieces, and sell those pieces as parts of the Brooklyn bridge. Not only was he getting free product inventory, but he also generated a lot of press for himself.

Try to think of how to do something that creates a good and exciting headline for whatever you are doing, which will grab people's attention.

7. Classifieds newspaper ads

Classified ads can be purchased in local or national newspapers. As you can imagine, the reach and cost would vary greatly. Local papers would charge you from one to few hundred dollars, and national newspapers can be as costly as tens of thousands of dollars per a single ad. You can also advertise in daily vs. weekly publications. Obviously weekly publications will be cheaper.

What you must do is experiment with ads that will work in a local weekly publication since they are the cheapest. To maximize your experimentation, you can try advertising in many different local newspapers at the same time to see which ad has better conversion.

One challenge is measuring how your classifieds ads actually convert. Many of your customers never tell you how they found your business. So you might never know if someone came from a classifieds ad. What you must do is give people either unique phone number line to call, or a unique discount code or a unique website page to visit so that you can know that everyone coming or calling through that is from a specific classifieds ad.

Another thing to keep in mind is what kind of a demographic you will be reaching. Very few kinds of people actually read classifieds ads. Most of the people who read newspapers these days tend to be over the age of 40 or 45 and older. They may also be the kinds of people who resist technological change.

8. Direct snail mail advertising

Even in this digital age, you still get companies mailing you physical letters for promotions, right? There are fewer such mailings, and they typically only come from a few types of companies. That should be a sign for you as to what kind of companies can be effectively promoted with direct snail mail, and whether your business fits into the profile of such a company.

Generally, if your business is a commonly used local business like a store or a restaurant, you can try to send people in your neighborhood promotions by regular snail mail just like you might slip flyers or brochures under their doors.

Keep in mind that there is a cost to sending or handing out every brochure, direct mailing or flyer. So only promote your business this way if it is something that gets you results and you can measure those results in the ways that I described earlier.

Rule of thumb: if you can't measure results of any paid promotion, you truly have no idea whether that promotion is profitable or whether you are losing money on it.

9. Cold calling and phone sales

To start with cold calling you need a great sales pitch, and luckily if you have gotten to this part of the book, you already have one.

The next thing you need is to figure out who will do the calling. I have hired telemarketers on Fiverr.com in the past who can call 15 numbers for about $5, but that is the cheapest it can go.

When cold calling, you must have the conversation mapped out in advance to account for the most common answers someone can give you, and have a response to every non-optimal answer.

Finding the numbers to call can also be a challenge. If you are selling to businesses, their phone numbers are easy to collect because they all have websites where they readily post their phone numbers.

If you are calling individual consumers, there are two strategies for getting their phone numbers. The first is going to annoy people in a major way, but it will enable you to reach thousands of people. It is by pre-loading the phone book's list of phone numbers to an automated software that automatically calls people one by one, and tells them about your offer. 95% of the people who will be called will absolutely hate that you are sending them automated voice messages and automated phone calls, but a small percentage of the people whom you call this way will engage with whatever you are offering. The other way to get people's phone numbers is to buy lists of consumer phone numbers for consumers who fit the target demographics of the kinds of consumers that you are targeting.

10. Storefront without a storefront

A storefront is something that brick and mortar businesses have. It is a part of the building that faces a street with a window. This window allows people who walk by the business to peek inside, learn about the business, and hopefully take an interest. In many cases the window of the store is the A of AIDA as it is meant to grab people's attention.

If you are opening a physical location for your business, a really big part of the decision as to where to open it would be to find a location which has a big storefront on a street which gets a lot of foot traffic.

But what if you don't have a storefront in case your business is a website or another business which doesn't have a physical location other than your home or some tucked-away office?

If you don't have a readily available storefront, you can artificially manufacture one by setting up a cart or a stand or a kiosk or a truck with big signs, logos and your URL somewhere on a busy street with lots of passer-by foot traffic. This way you can actually make some sales while getting many people who don't initially engage to at least notice and become familiar with your business. That familiarity will increase the chances that next time they pass by and see your business they might engage.

11. Setting up a cart or a stand or selling at flea markets or fairs

Taking off from the previous section's idea of setting up a storefront, you can also try to sell your products or promote your business at flea markets, fairs or similar events. If you are not familiar with what flea markets are, they are basically large places where many small businesses gather to sell or promote their goods to people who are looking for unique items or discounts. Every large city has fairs and flea markets.

Try to find what fairs or flea markets are going on in the nearby cities and towns near you, and try to promote whatever your business sells there.

All you need to do is invest in a portable chair, table and nice signs so that your business looks attractive, and you will be able to drum up some sales anywhere you set up your basic stand.

The End

Best of luck promoting your business! I wish you amazing success in everything you do, and really hope that the strategies in this book bring you tremendous profits.

ADDITIONAL BOOKS THAT MIGHT HELP YOU

Here is a link to my Amazon author profile with a full list of my 20 books:

https://goo.gl/NB1iXk

This link redirects to the .com version of the link. If you are in UK or other European countries, please change the .com to your country's appropriate country setting for this link to work.

FURTHER FREE RESOURCES

Gift 1: I will give you one free online business/marketing course of YOUR choosing and huge discounts on any additional courses.

I teach over 100 online courses on business and marketing. I will give you one of the courses for absolutely free, and you can choose which one. Browse my full list of courses and email me telling me which course you want, and I will send you a free coupon!

Here is my full list of courses:

https://www.udemy.com/user/alexgenadinik/

Just send me an email to alex.genadinik@gmail.com and tell me that you got this book, and which of my courses you would like for free, and I will send you a coupon code to get that course for free.

Gift: 2: Get my Android and iPhone business apps for free.

You can find all my free apps on my website:

http://www.problemio.com

Here are some of my individual apps. The apps come as a 4-app course and on Android I have free versions of each!

Free business plan app:
https://play.google.com/store/apps/details?id=com.problemio&hl=en

Free marketing app:
https://play.google.com/store/apps/details?id=com.marketing&hl=en

Free app on fundraising and making money:
https://play.google.com/store/apps/details?id=make.money&hl=en

Free business idea app:
https://play.google.com/store/apps/details?id=business.ideas&hl=en

Gift 3: Free business advice

If you have questions about your events, your overall business, or anything mentioned in this book, email me at alex.genadinik@gmail.com and I will be happy to help you. Just please keep two things in mind:

1) Remind me that you got this book and that you are not just a random person on the Internet.
2) Please make the questions clear and short. I love to help, but I am often overwhelmed with work, and always short on the time that I have available.

COMPLETE LIST OF MY BOOKS

If you enjoyed this book, check out my author page to see the full list of my books:
http://www.amazon.com/Alex-Genadinik/e/B00I114WEU

Thank you for reading and please keep in touch!

ABOUT THE AUTHOR

Alex Genadinik is a software engineer, successful entrepreneur, and a marketer. Alex is a 3-time best selling Amazon author, and the creator of the Problemio.com business apps which are some of the top mobile apps for planning and starting a business with 1,000,000 downloads across iOS, Android and Kindle. Alex has a B.S in Computer Science from San Jose State University.

Alex is also a prominent online teacher, and loves to help entrepreneurs achieve their dreams.

Made in the USA
San Bernardino, CA
04 April 2019